Don't Slurp Your Soup

*A long overdue book which is
necessary reading for any
business professional.*

Larry Wilson, CEO
Pecos River Learning Center
Coauthor
The One Minute Salesperson

A Basic Guide to Business Etiquette

Elizabeth Craig

Brighton Publications, Inc.

Printed in the United States of America

"We work daily in situations where lack of knowledge of the basics of business etiquette can jeopardize important business relationships. *Don't Slurp Your Soup* offers advice and direction for virtually any situation."

—Thomas P. Caine
Chairman of the Board
CGMS Incorporated
National Financial Consulting Firm

"*Don't Slurp Your Soup, A Basic Guide to Business Etiquette* has an extremely well written and necessary chapter on international etiquette. Every American businessperson must know the information contained in this chapter before traveling abroad. Comprehensive yet brief, the international chapter provides the businessperson with 'the one-minute introduction to foreign travel.' Practice the information provided and businesspeople around the world will believe you are competent and able to do the job."

—Gerhard (Gary) E. Schwämmlein
Director of Corporate Planning
Monsanto Company
St. Louis, Missouri

"Elizabeth Craig handles social situations with such style and confidence! Now, she's put it all in a book that's easy to use. Anyone following her helpful guide will always put their best foot forward."

—Kay Emel-Powell
Product Team Leader
Betty Crocker Food & Publications Center
General Mills, Inc.

Brighton Publications, Inc.

Copyright © 1991, revised 1996 by Elizabeth L. Craig

Brighton Publications, Inc.
P.O. Box 120706
St. Paul, MN 55112-0706
612-636-2220

First Edition: 1991
Second Edition: 1996

Library of Congress Cataloging-in-Publication Data

Craig, Elizabeth
    Don't slurp your soup : a basic guide to business etiquette / Elizabeth Craig. — 2nd rev. ed.
        p.   cm.
    ISBN 0-918420-26-1
    1. Business etiquette. I. Title.
HF5389.C73   1996
395' .52 — dc20   96-11547
                                                          CIP

ISBN 0-918420-26-1

Printed in the United States of America

Contents

Introduction

Executives from a Fortune 100 company, one of America's largest corporations, take potential employees to lunch or dinner to observe their comfort level with spouses, servers, and yes, even multiple pieces of tableware. Etiquette does play a major role in the business world.

Like it or not, good manners at the workplace are associated with competence in business. Likewise, sloppy manners are equated with lack of ability. On any given day, a business professional may need to know how to make group introductions, how to carry on appropriate conversations at a business lunch, or how to host an event attended by international guests.

Because business is competitive in our global economy, business professionals must seize every opportunity to favorably distinguish themselves and their employers from those of their competitors. It is important to understand the culture and local custom of international business associates. As an example, slurping soup is not considered good manners in the United States but is proper in Japan, China, and other Asian countries.

In business, many times a front-line employee may be a company's only contact with clients or customers. It is to everyone's benefit for that person to have access to appropriate business etiquette information.

Etiquette often is simply common sense. Yet common sense is not always common information. This guide is meant to give the busy professional answers to the situations encountered in daily working life. Many professionals, although experts in their field, experience embarrassing moments simply from not knowing what behavior is appropriate. Etiquette does make a difference.

Elizabeth L. Craig

1 Office Etiquette

Let's face it. Even today, with new emphasis on restoring balance to people's lives, businesspeople still spend long hours at the office. Many workers spend more of their waking hours at work than at home. But, just as you need to strive to achieve harmony within your family, you need to work hard—if not harder—to create friendly, professional relationships among your co-workers. Some businesspeople claim that "getting along at the office is half the job." Whether or not this is true, your workdays will speed along more quickly and you'll get more done if you and your co-workers have congenial working relationships. Using good office etiquette not only helps make the atmosphere in your office more pleasant and productive, but it also can help you move up at promotion time.

DEPARTMENT MEETINGS

Meetings are a fact of business life. Your knowledge of how to conduct yourself at meetings is a measure of your business competence. The first rule of meeting etiquette is *always arrive on time*.

If you are leading the meeting, always circulate a meeting agenda beforehand to everyone who will be attending. One thing I do when preparing an agenda is to put all the *action* items first, then the *discussion* items, and then all the items of *information*, such as the date, time, and place of other related upcoming meetings. By putting the action items first—those items that require some decision at the meeting—you encourage people to arrive on time.

If you are asked to attend the meeting, be sure to read the agenda and bring all the papers you'll need. When seated, sit up straight and act interested. Maintain eye contact with whomever is speaking and avoid getting into conversation with others seated near you.

Introductions in business situations are very important, especially at meetings. If introductions have not been made, help everyone feel comfortable by making sure everyone is introduced. Making sure everyone knows one another helps groups function more cohesively. If you're the person who doesn't get introduced, take the initiative to introduce yourself. If you are the chairperson of the meeting and time permits, go around the table and ask everyone to introduce himself or herself. Sometimes this is best done just before the first break, since some people may arrive late.

If you absolutely cannot arrive on time, there are a few ways you can ease your way into the meeting room. First, get ready before you enter the room. Take out the agenda, your note pad, and your pen so that you're ready to write. Enter as quietly and unobtrusively as possible. Forget about taking any food or coffee with you when you are late. Look around quickly as you enter to locate an open seat. If there are no assigned seats, select one close to the door. If all those seats are taken, take the nearest seat, even if it is near the speaker.

If you won't be interrupting anyone's presentation, apologize for your lateness, but do not offer excuses or explain why you were late. If you feel there is a need, offer an explanation when it's your turn to speak. If you haven't gotten ready as suggested before entering the room, quickly take the items you'll need from your briefcase. Avoid bringing unnecessary papers that you'll have to shuffle through. An effective technique to allow you to get right into the flow of the meeting is to have all your notes organized beforehand according to the agenda. Note on your agenda where you have something to say. Jump right into the meeting; if your colleagues are on agenda item 3 and you have something to say, say it.

If you must leave a meeting early, make sure to tell the chairperson beforehand. It's sometimes a good idea to call the week before and let the chairperson know of your plans. Bring as few things as possible with you to make your getaway easier. Sit as close to the door as possible. Leave quietly, and by all means don't let the door slam behind you.

Another aspect of meeting etiquette is to follow the style of the meeting's leader. This means that if everyone is joining in freely with ideas, feel free to jump in with yours. On the other hand, before you jump in, make sure you have something worthwhile to say. Otherwise, it's best to remain silent. When working as a member of a group, take credit only for those things that are yours. When your statements represent the views of a group, be a "we" person, not an "I" person.

Leading meetings successfully is an important business skill. In addition to mastering the mechanics of conducting meetings, it is advantageous to learn about the personalities of others. You will need to learn how to help some people make their contributions shorter, and to ask others for suggestions if they don't contribute freely. Remember—the purpose of a meeting is to bring a group together to accomplish what individuals cannot accomplish alone. Meeting etiquette requires that you respect each person's contribution. To gain more insight on how you can become a better meeting leader or participant, check your local library's business section for books on this topic.

The place you choose to sit at a meeting can be very important. Some authorities on the subject recommend that you position yourself directly across from the person of importance. However, I have found that sitting across from a person encourages conflict. People who sit side by side tend to support each another's ideas. So when you need a person to support a great idea of yours, be sure to sit next to him. He may be surprised when you do this, but at least while he's wondering what's going on, he may not disagree with your idea.

The location of your seat in a meeting is more important than most people ever imagine. The hierarchy of seating goes from left to right. Generally, you want to sit to the immediate left of the person who has the most influence in the meeting. Be aware that this is not always the person who is leading the meeting. Housekeeping tasks are usually given to the person to the right of the chairperson. So unless you really want to be the meeting's custodian, choose another seat. If you are unable to sit to the left of the person with the most influence, consider sitting at a corner of the table. Why? When you do so, you seem to take up more physical space. When you occupy more physical space, you have a more powerful presence, and thus you seem to wield greater influence. This is different from sitting next to empty chairs, which is something I do not recommend. Sitting next to an empty chair takes away your influence, since the physical space is not filled. The United States/Vietnam Peace Conference of 1972 illustrates just how important seating can be. One of the most time consuming and difficult details in preparing for the conference was the extensive discussion that took place over the shape of the conference table and the seating arrangement. Where each person sat was considered very important to the success of the negotiations.

Besides arriving on time and being prepared for the meeting, plan to make at least one statement or ask one question. This will highlight your visibility. If someone else in the meeting takes an idea you presented earlier and claims it as their own, remind people that you had the original idea. What is the most diplomatic way to do this? I've said things like, "Ed, I'm so glad you picked up on the idea I had. Some ideas I had for carrying it out were . . . . "

One important but sometimes overlooked piece of advice regarding meetings is *treat everyone equally*. Pay the same amount of attention to the person with the least senior position as you do to the person with the most authority. Don't try to butter up the person you think is the most important. And remember that the youngest person of the group isn't necessarily the one with the least senior position.

Responding inappropriately to a person's age, sex, or professional position can hamper your business growth. Usually you will want to defer to your superiors. This means standing when they enter your office, letting them tell you where to sit when in someone else's office or in a meeting, and letting them be seated first in a car. Be sure to thank them after they offer you a chair or suggest where you may sit. You also should defer to all people who visit your office by standing when they enter and when they leave.

PERFORMANCE REVIEWS

Receiving a performance review from a supervisor can make anyone nervous. But to calm your jitters, simply make sure you are adequately prepared for the meeting. You may be asked to complete a variety of forms or answer questions about your performance objectives and goals. Come prepared with examples to discuss your accomplishments. Maintain good eye contact, be open to criticism and suggestions for improvement, and remember that performance reviews are give-and-take situations. Be prepared to give your supervisor good, honest feedback on her performance, too.

What a feeling of relief and accomplishment an excellent review brings. To show your appreciation to your manager for rating your performance so highly, you might be tempted to respond with a gift. While it's a thoughtful idea, it's not a smart business move. Your reasons for giving a gift to your boss on this occasion may well be misinterpreted. If you feel very strongly about giving a gift, wait for a more appropriate occasion such as a birthday or a holiday. Even when giving a gift then, make it a small, inexpensive one, and something for the office. Appropriate gifts in this situation include such things as a pen set or a paperweight. The best way to show your appreciation is to simply express your thanks for the glowing review and let your supervisor know that what you've learned from working with him or her has had a positive effect on your performance.

SUPERVISING PEERS

Supervising those who were your peers before your promotion requires some tact and consideration. When you are promoted, relationships change. Although making the transition can be a challenge, you can take some steps to make it more smoothly. Start off on the right foot by holding a meeting during which you and your staff discuss each person's responsibilities and expectations. Stressing that you're all still working together for the benefit of the company and that you value their input will help eliminate feelings of jealousy or resentment. Even though you may not want to stop being their friend, your relationship probably will change. Remember that you are no longer one of them, and it is inappropriate for you to get involved in all their office conversations. Playing favorites also will make the situation even more tense than it might already be. Let it be known that you're willing to discuss any concerns your former peers may have.

SIX STEPS TO DELEGATING

Delegating is a particularly important skill to master when you supervise others. If you can delegate successfully, you can get more done, and you can get it done correctly the first time.

The first step is to explain *why* the job is important.

Second, you want to describe the *exact results* you are after. This seems very obvious, but I know of an office manager who asked her assistant to alphabetize her card file. The assistant, very logically, filed each person's card by the last name. The office manager had not mentioned that what she wanted was for the accounts to be indexed by company name. It took more time to undo this situation than it would have taken to do the job correctly the first time.

The third step to effective delegating is to define what *authority* the person has. Is the person assigned to a project allowed to have four hours of a particular engineer's time to get necessary data? Let the person know what authority, if any, they have to get the job done.

The fourth step is very important to completing the project on time: Agree on a *deadline*. In fact, after defining the scope of a project, I often start by asking the person when they think they can have the project completed. Often they will tell me a date that is one week sooner than the date I would have set. Sometimes, if I feel their date is unrealistic, we go over the time together to make sure they have accurately calculated the time they need to complete the project. A delegate who is involved in deciding the deadline feels much more responsible for completing the project by the agreed-on due date.

The fifth step to effective delegating is asking for *feedback*. Ask the person to give you feedback throughout the project. Let them know you don't want any surprises when the project is due. The fifth and sixth steps go hand in hand. The sixth step is to provide for *check points* along the way. Having mini due dates or check points allows you to ensure that the entire project will be completed by the deadline.

OFFICE VISITORS

When bringing visitors to your office, you must decide whether or not it is appropriate to meet with them there. It may be better to meet in a conference room. Why? You may be working on a project that is confidential. If you do have to meet with visitors in your office, take an extra five to ten minutes to look around your office and put away anything that you wouldn't want someone else to see. Have bins and drawers in your office to throw confidential information into.

When you do have scheduled visitors to your office, not only should you stand to greet them, but you also must put aside anything else you're doing. This includes ending a phone conversation. Doing this requires some finesse, so you don't offend one or both parties. If someone does enter while you're on the phone, stand and smile to greet her and show her where she may be seated. While you're doing this, explain to the person on the phone that you have a visitor and will get back to him when possible. Those who are there in person usually have priority over those present in voice only. You, of course, will need to evaluate each situation as it arises.

OFFICE NOISE

If anyone has ever told you that your voice carries, you should consider how loudly you speak in all sorts of business situations and work to modulate your voice. It is particularly important in "open" offices that have cubicles. In this type of office, just about everything you do and say in your office can be heard by someone else. Appropriate office etiquette tells you that if you're talking on your telephone or greeting someone, you must talk as quietly as possible. Whenever possible, meet with visitors in conference rooms. This also gives you the privacy you may need so that others in your offices aren't privy to confidential information.

APPROPRIATE LANGUAGE

Use of appropriate language in business is important. Although you may not be embarrassed by the way you speak, talking in an unbusinesslike way or using slang may prevent you from being accepted in business. Saying things like "Ain't dat right?" in business often makes one sound unintelligent. You're an educated person in a professional office, so search your vocabulary and find appropriate words to express yourself. Also, there is no acceptable reason for anyone in an office, especially a manager, to use obscenity.

A word of caution for businessmen: Watch the language you use when addressing female professionals. The secretarial pool is not "the girls," and a businesswoman is not "honey." Implying that a woman got a deal settled because she's female and making other sexist remarks are definitely out of line, even if said jokingly. Avoid using "ladies," as it can be understood as belittling or patronizing; use "women," instead.

HUMOR IN THE WORKPLACE

Being humorous can be an important skill in business if the humor is used in a humane and positive way. If you want to develop positive humor skills, you may even be able to find a course that teaches this type of humor. Still, be aware that ethnic, racial, and gender jokes that used to be considered funny are no longer appropriate. Any joke that carries these overtones probably will backfire. Be very careful with any humor to be sure it really is funny and not hurtful to anyone, or you may be criticized for being insulting.

Not only will you want to choose your jokes carefully, you should only kid those people you know well. What one person finds amusing can be quite offensive to another. If the joke is hurtful to anyone in any way, do not use it. The disclaimer "I'm just kidding" doesn't work any longer.

Probably the safest humor is making fun of yourself. Most people don't take offense at this, but be careful not to belittle or downgrade yourself and negatively affect your image.

Several colleges and universities have voted to prohibit the use of any language that stigmatizes or victimizes people based on race, religion, gender, sexual orientation, disability, weight, height, and a host of other traits. In some companies, a first-time offender is given a warning. A second offense carries up to a $100 fine.

OFFICE THEFT

Being polite and remembering your office etiquette is more challenging in some situations than in others. One such instance is when you know someone is "permanently borrowing" something from the company. You don't want to accuse her of committing a crime, and yet you know you should say something to someone.

As difficult as it might be for you to turn this person in to the appropriate higher authority, it is necessary that you do so immediately. If this person's actions are later discovered and it is found that you knew about her activities all along but didn't do anything about it, you may have just put your job in jeopardy.

Another tricky situation is when one of your associates is giving you false information to make you look bad. This is a situation in which you'd better make sure the person is actually guilty. Both of your reputations are on the line here. Confront him personally with your concerns and suspicions. If you can't settle the issue between the two of you, take it to the appropriate higher authority. Still, don't go to your superior shouting accusations and swearing that your associate is guilty. Calmly and coolly presenting the situation and letting your associate give his side of the story is the most diplomatic way to handle it.

Office Furniture

Many companies spend much money on office furniture, believing this is an important part of an employee's work environment. One owner of a major public relations firm spent approximately $5,000 per office cubicle on furniture only to find that these items were not being cared for properly. Hot and cold drinks were set on desktops instead of on the coasters that were provided, leaving permanent ring marks on the top. In the conference room, pizzas were set in the middle of the wooden table, leaving large, permanent white marks.

Would you ever put your feet up on the coffee table in an office waiting room? Some people do—even while waiting to be interviewed for a job. Think before you make yourself too comfortable and cost yourself a job.

Desk Privacy

Your desk is as neat as can be and you can hardly bear the "mess" on your neighbor's desk. No matter how unorganized your peer's desk may look or how well your system works for you, resist the temptation to rearrange, clean off, or otherwise disturb someone else's desk. People can become very defensive when others straighten their papers and rearrange their drawers. It might be a mess, but it's an "organized mess." Since it isn't interfering with her performance, hurting the company's image, or bothering her supervisor or others, you'll just have to live with your messy neighbor. If she wants your help or advice on being better organized, she will ask for it.

OFFICE ETIQUETTE POINTERS

Here are some office etiquette pointers to keep in mind:

◄ Addressing your supervisor or client by the first name without having permission to do so does not show your business sense. Unless told otherwise, address these people by their formal title.

◄ Be sure to return RSVPs promptly.

◄ The two most important phrases you'll ever use in business are "Thank you" and "I apologize." They say more about your manners and professionalism than you may realize. It's not always enough just to say them. Sometimes handwritten notes are appropriate.

◄ Show compassion and concern for a colleague or associate who has lost a loved one by sending a note of condolence.

◄ If you must keep someone who has arrived on time for his appointment waiting, be sure to acknowledge his presence by greeting him, then apologizing for and explaining the delay. If you can't greet him personally, have your secretary explain to him that you know he is there and that you will be with him shortly.

2 Everyday Professional Behavior

Everyone knows that professional behavior in the office is expected. But being well behaved in the office doesn't mean you can act otherwise when you are away from the office. Your behavior in associates' offices and at business functions reflects not only on yourself but also on your company.

THE HANDSHAKE

Do not underestimate the importance of an appropriate businesslike handshake. Since the first edition of this book came out, one of the most asked questions from businesspeople is, "How is my handshake?" A handshake is a big part of making a positive first impression.

A firm, assertive handshake is a business asset. Handshakes make a difference, because you remember people longer if you shake hands with them. Shake hands so that the "web" between your thumb and index finger meet firmly with the other person's. Shake hands firmly, and with only one squeeze. Pump up and down only once or twice. As you shake someone's hand, also make eye contact. A limp handshake can be interpreted as weakness, indecisiveness, or a lack of enthusiasm. A squeeze that lasts too long can say, "I'm in charge." A damp palm can indicate nervousness. And while we're on the subject, please note: There are firm handshakes and there are FIRM handshakes. A tight, vicelike handshake may unintentionally signal too much aggressiveness. Shake hands firmly, but not so firmly that you hurt someone's hand. It should be firm enough to display your sense of confidence without being a bone crusher. If you're shaking hands with someone whose body weight is much less than yours, then lighten up! Guaranteed—the person will appreciate your consideration. Two-handed shakes, though they exhibit warmth, are not considered appropriate in business situations.

The person who initiates a handshake typically shows more confidence and control of a situation. Treat men and women with equal respect. A man no longer has to wait for a woman to extend her hand. Either the man or woman may offer their hand first. When meeting a dignitary or a person with a disability, it's most considerate to let that person offer their hand first, regardless of gender. You can't be sure whether an elderly person or person with a disability is physically able to shake hands.

Seminar participants also commonly ask, "how long should a handshake last?" Generally speaking, a handshake should last only as long as it takes to greet the person. As mentioned earlier this typically means pumping up and down only once or twice.

If you are at a function where nametags are worn, always wear the tag on your right side, and keep it up towards your shoulder. When you shake hands with your right hand, the person you are meeting will automatically be drawn to that side to read your name. Otherwise the person with whom you're shaking hands has to look across and break eye contact with you for more than a second or two. Either they will not take time to look at your name tag, or they may appear shifty-eyed. Wearing your name tag on the right side eliminates a lot of awkwardness.

WHAT ABOUT "CHIVALRY"?

Traditionally, men have been taught to open doors for women, help them on with their coats, and step aside to let them exit elevators first. With more women entering the work force, it has become increasingly difficult for men (especially traditionally oriented ones) to know when they should and should not do these things for women. The best advice we can give businessmen is to treat the women in your office as your colleagues and save traditional manners for women outside the office. This means that when men are with a female colleague, they no longer have to feel obligated to open doors for her, assist her with her coat, carry her packages, let her out of the elevator first, or pay for her lunch. Women can do these things for themselves. Treat your female colleagues with the same respect and regard you reserve for your male colleagues. The person who gets to the door first should open it. If a man approaching a door has his arms full, it would be extremely impolite for a woman not to open it for him if she is standing nearby. It's common politeness for both sexes to help a peer whenever they need it. You will be amazed at the wonderful treatment you'll receive in return when you treat everyone as the chief executive officer of a major firm.

COMPLIMENTS

A safe route to travel regarding compliments is to not compliment a business associate on his or her appearance. However, you should take into account the corporate culture of the company for which your associate works. For example, an advertising agency often has a very visual image to project, and a compliment such as "Nice tie" may be appropriate. If you work at a law firm with a staid reputation, it may be considered very unprofessional to comment on appearance. Remember that compliments about one's appearance, however innocent, could be misconstrued.

It is often best to limit comments in the office and at business functions to work-related items. Comment only about such things as an excellent question, a good point made in a meeting, a job well done, or a thorough analysis on a project. Businesswomen should take a professional compliment from a businessman for what it is, and businessmen shouldn't worry that a compliment they give will be misconstrued.

Businesswomen have some control over how much respect they receive at the office. To be treated as professionals, they must behave professionally. This means not applying makeup or hair spray at the desk. Hand lotion is fine as long as it isn't too strongly scented. Proper attire is a given.

ADDRESSING WOMEN

Many people are unsure just how to address women in the work force. Is "Mrs.," "Miss," or "Ms." proper?. Unless you're sure that a woman prefers to be addressed as "Miss" or "Mrs.," avoid using these titles. They are considered unbusinesslike. As a rule, addressing any businesswoman as "Ms." is the preferred route.

The "Mrs./Ms." issue can be a problem when addressing envelopes. The best way to address an envelope is to put the woman's first and last name only on the outside envelope and then put "Ms." first and her last name on the letter itself. When writing to someone whose gender you're not sure of, begin your letter with "Dear Sir or Madam."

If you want to be sure how a woman prefers to be addressed, call her office and ask the receptionist or secretary if she has a preference. If a person's name doesn't indicate whether the person is male or female, call their secretary and ask.

ELEVATOR ETIQUETTE

You know how it is when you're in an elevator. You get in, push the button for your floor, and then stare at the door or at the floor numbers above it while the elevator takes you to your destination. But there are a few things to keep in mind about elevator etiquette.

If the up or down arrow is already lit and someone is waiting for the elevator when you get there, don't press the button for the elevator again. Believe me, that is not going to make it get there any quicker.

To make everyone's ride more comfortable, do refrain from staring at others. Focus on a spot on the door, look at the floor, read your report one last time—do anything except stare at others.

What do you do when you see someone sprinting for the elevator just as the door is closing? If there is room in the elevator, press the "Open Door" button and hold the door until the person has stepped in. If the elevator is already full, squeezing in another person probably isn't the best idea.

Be sensitive about talking in an elevator. Especially when you are riding with co-workers, take extra care in choosing topics of conversation. Avoid bringing up confidential subjects. Silence in the elevator is probably best. If you must talk, do so softly.

If you're in the back of the elevator when you reach your floor, a clearly announced "Excuse me, please" is sufficient notice for everyone to clear a path for you. If you're in the front when others behind you are trying to exit, step out of the elevator (be sure to hold the door open!) and let them pass. If a man and woman are getting out on the same floor and the man is closer to the door, there is no reason for him to step aside and let the woman exit first.

ESCALATOR ETIQUETTE

Proper escalator etiquette calls for a single file of standees on the right side of the moving stairs, and an open passing lane on the left. Otherwise fast walkers will pull up behind side-by-siders, sigh and roll their eyes. These fast walkers are in a hurry and will be irritated wondering if you are deliberately trying to slow them down.

Another point of escalator etiquette is once you step off the escalator keep walking. For some reason people tend to stop after stepping off the escalator, particularly side-by-siders who continue their conversations stopped at the exit from the escalator. This gives the individuals after them very little if any space to step off. Continuing to move after you exit the escalator is not only a matter of common sense and consideration, but a safety issue.

PROFESSIONAL DRESS

Take the phrase "dress for success" very seriously. How you dress in the corporate world is very important, because it makes a statement about you and affects everyone you meet. Dressing inappropriately for your position can prevent you from getting the promotion you deserve, though you'll probably never know that this was the real reason. It's hard to be the president of the company or even a representative of it if you wear out-of-date suits and ties that clash.

Two-piece suits seem to be the the the most acceptable dress for women professionals, although suit dresses are popular, also. Low-cut and sheer clothing will diminish women's chances of a dream job just as quickly. Remember that people still judge a book by its cover. All of those corny adages like, "You'll never get a second chance to make a first impression" are still true. People form a first impression in the first 7 to 30 seconds of meeting you. And, it's been found that it is difficult to change a first impression. Together with business etiquette, professional appearance has a big impact on your career success.

Men should pay particular attention to the shirts they wear. Short-sleeved shirts are fine if you plan to leave your suit coat on. In certain corporate cultures, a short-sleeved shirt and tie may not give a professional appearance. But, in other professions, short-sleeved shirts and ties are acceptable. Some say short-sleeved shirts are never appropriate for men in business situations. Look around and see what is acceptable in your industry and company culture. However, don't lower your ideals of what is appropriate just because other people don't meet up to them. If you are more comfortable dressing a little more formally, then do so. But be careful not to overdress.

Every company has an unwritten dress code. Sometimes companies located downtown have a more formal dress code than those in the suburbs. You may dress less formally in your own office than you would when visiting other businesses. Figure out as quickly as possible the most appropriate professional dress for each business situation.

To dress "in casual attire" for the company picnic, find out more specifically what "casual attire" really means. A fifty-year-old man may interpret casual dress to mean that he doesn't have to wear a tie. A twenty-year-old may believe that casual dress means a swimming suit or cut-offs and T-shirt. Different generations interpret things differently. A few companies have learned that employees appreciate specific descriptions. For a company retreat, one firm put the following in their conference memo: "Casual attire is recommended (i.e., casual pants, cords, sweaters—preferably no ties or jeans)." Check with others in the firm to find out how "casual attire" is defined for each business function you attend.

In the early-1990s a trend towards Fridays being "casual dress" day came into vogue. By the mid-1990s this translated to "business casual dress" being appropriate every day of the week. About two-thirds of American companies allow casual or business casual clothing in the office on a seasonal basis, or on designated "casual days." These companies are from a variety of industries and represent all regions of the United States. What this new trend toward continuous five-day business casual really did was create a great deal of confusion about how a person was supposed to dress for work. As a result some companies set up task forces to conduct surveys which were used as the basis for establishing company positions on the "business casual dress" issue. Business casual clothing encompasses many looks, but it really means casual clothing that is appropriate for an office environment. It is clothing that allows you to feel comfortable at work, yet always looks neat and professional, providing a positive image for customers and visitors. Business casual is applicable to some industries, but not all business situations. Think about each day's activities when determining what to wear. Formal business dress is always acceptable and may be required when meeting with customers or visitors.

If you prefer to work without your coat, be sure to put it on when a superior or visitor comes to your office, and leave it on until he or she leaves. Also, wear your coat whenever you are walking around the office in public areas. The rule of thumb is: Whenever you are going to be seen, put your coat on. Suit coats must be worn in meetings unless the leader suggests that it's all right to remove them.

Personal hygiene is always of the utmost importance. Be clean and fresh smelling at all times. Arrange your hair in a becoming style and get rid of dandruff. Use cologne or perfume sparingly, if at all. Too much is never appropriate.

Having to work with someone who neglects personal hygiene is no fun. Ask your supervisor to approach the person about the problem.

You may want to avoid fashion trends such as bleaching one section of your hair, wearing a pony tail, or piercing an ear, if you are a man. In some professions this is fine; in other areas of the business world it is not appropriate.

BODY LANGUAGE

Your body language may be even more important than your attire. Body language tells people a lot about how you are feeling and thinking. Using positive body language in addition to correct manners gives you the confidence to succeed. People with positive self-esteem are those people who can achieve the highest levels of success in their personal and professional lives.

An example of positive body language is entering a room with a smile and good posture. These project an image of readiness and self-confidence. Be ready to offer a firm, friendly handshake. Make eye contact when you shake hands and whenever you are listening to someone else talk.

Everyone likes to maintain a certain zone of space around herself. In business situations, it is appropriate to maintain six-to eight-foot distance from your listener. If six feet is too far for you, it's fine to move closer, but no closer than an arm's length away.

THIRD-PARTY INFORMATION

Whenever you're asked for information about another person, be very careful about what you say. If you are asked to provide information that you feel is confidential, respond by saying something like, "I feel that information is confidential. It is not appropriate for me to provide it to you." Some people may continue to push you for information that you really think you should not give. Stay firm about your decision not to answer. You might offer to discuss it with the person you are being asked to divulge information about. That person can respond directly to the person inquiring if they are willing to share the information.

If you need time to think, say something like, "I feel that information may be confidential. I'll call you back." Take the time you need to check with appropriate people, such as your human resources department, and consider what information, if any, you will provide.

You may be held legally responsible for whatever you say about another person. If something you say or write injures a person's professional standing, you may be sued. Wherever injury could result to one's reputation in any way, you should not make any comments, regardless of the truth. You walk a very fine line with laws regarding libel and slander. For a remark to be considered slanderous, it must be spoken to someone else or in the presence of another person. It is common sense not to talk about others. Say nothing if you are unable to be positive in your remarks.

Regarding personal and confidential information, treat others the same way you would like to be treated. I continue to be amazed by what a small world it really is and how fast information can be passed on. Don't gossip about a person's personal life. Gossiping is not professional, so don't accidently fall into this behavior even if a colleague does. The less you say to anyone concerning a third party—especially to a stranger on the telephone—the better.

Give yourself a self-test by asking the question: "Would I provide this information if it were going to be shown on the evening news, or appear in the next issue of the local paper, without my having a chance to explain?" Answering this question will help you sleep better at night.

RECOGNITION AND CONGRATULATIONS

As any professional businessperson knows, it is very important for you to stay in touch with your clients and associates throughout the year. In addition to sending a card during the holidays, consider other ways to keep in touch. When someone you know is promoted or honored, or when you see them featured in a newspaper article, drop them a note. Carefully cut out the article, use glue stick to attach it to an informal business note card, and handwrite a note of congratulations or a note such as "I saw you in the news and thought you might want another copy." Keeping in touch in this way shows people you know what is going on and that you care about them personally.

BEREAVEMENT ETIQUETTE

Before the Funeral

Funeral customs vary according to the religious and other preferences of the bereaved. If you are uncertain about what to do, call the funeral home to check on the appropriate procedures to follow. The following are some hints to get you started.

As soon as possible, send a message of condolence. This is preferable to placing a telephone call. Only those closest to the family of the deceased should phone. In a business situation, an executive can dictate a note from the company. However, a typed note to a close friend is not appropriate; a short, handwritten message is proper in this situation.

Use personal judgment to choose the route you feel is appropriate to relay personal condolences. If the funeral is large, the bereaved will probably receive duplicates of the same printed sympathy card. For this reason, type or handwrite a note on your personal stationary.

Relating a personal memory you have of the deceased or how they positively influenced your life is often appreciated by the family.
Here is an example of a personal note to express sympathy:

> Dear Michael,
>> I was so sorry to hear your sad news.
>> Your loss is so personal that only you feel its full measure. So although I can't know fully how you feel, I want you to know I am thinking about you.
>> Memories of those we love live on and never die. Susan's life will always touch yours as she lives on in your memory and in the memories of all others who knew her. Along with sympathy, I send understanding and encouragement.
>
> Warm regards,
>
> Elizabeth Jones

Flowers may be sent to the church, the family's home, or the grave site, but you will want to abide by the family's wishes as to whether they want flowers at all. Often the immediate family may purchase a few floral arrangements and request that others give memorials instead. If flowers are sent from a place of business, a white card with one line of condolences and the company's name must accompany the flowers.

A memorial may be given to an organization or charity of your choice. Mail a check to the organization, along with a note giving the name and address of family or bereaved, and also your name as the donor. The organization will send an acknowledgment to you that includes the amount donated. The designated relative will be notified that you have donated to their charity in the memory of the deceased, but the amount will not be disclosed.

The Funeral

Black is the traditional color of mourning, but many people opt to wear other colors to funerals. Women may want to wear a sedate color and avoid light or bright colors. Only conservative jewelry should be worn. Standard dress for men usually includes a dark suit and a conservative tie.

When entering the place where the service is being held, be sure to sign the guest book, usually located near the entrance. It is often a comfort to the family to know who came to pay their respects to the deceased.

The immediate family sits in the front seats. You may decide to be seated right away or stay near the entrance to greet others. The minister usually announces each event in the ceremony. If there is to be an open-casket viewing, the minister or other presider will announce it. It is your choice to view the body by filing past the casket or stopping briefly in front of it. If you do not wish to view the body, stay standing in the waiting area until the minister indicates that the funeral is to begin. Then you may seat yourself.

After the service is over, family members leave first, with other mourners following. Those people seated at the front leave first, and others follow row by row.

After the Funeral

Usually only family members go to the cemetery after the funeral, but others may be specifically asked to attend. Mourners except for the family use their cars and travel at a moderate speed. Headlights are turned on to show other motorists that the procession is moving as a group and has the right-of-way.

After the burial, there is usually a reception. This is typically open to all those who attended the funeral.

3 Telephone Fundamentals

Good telephone manners are not complicated to learn. But there are a few guidelines to follow when using the phone at the office and at home.

AT THE OFFICE

Wouldn't it be great if you could call a business and speak directly to the person you're calling without having to go through receptionists, voice mail, or answering machines? Unfortunately, in some businesses, such luck is a rarity.

Whenever possible, answer your phone yourself. It will impress your associates, customers, and clients, and your receptionist or secretary will love you for it. You may be surprised at how much more in touch you feel with what is going on in your business, in the world around you, and with your customers.

Some of my business associates ask their secretaries to take messages. They tell me that a secretary or assistant is best for taking messages, since they often can help the person immediately and there is no need for a return call. If the person can do additional duties, they can also schedule things and can help by getting files, or doing other tasks. Whoever answers the telephone for them is asked to take messages as detailed as possible. This way they are able to be prepared with any necessary information before returning the call.

One effective way to deal with telephone calls is to devote a portion of each day to returning ones you've received during the day. Some business associates of mine work on their top priorities from 8:00 A.M. until 11:00 A.M. Then they return their telephone calls at 11:00 A.M. and take all their own calls for the rest of the day. These businesspeople tell me that since they do the same thing every day, people learn to call them in the afternoon. This way they feel they have accomplished their priorities for the day before getting involved in new things. Good business etiquette dictates that all telephone calls be returned within 24 hours.

Since not all businesspeople are able to answer their own phones, it is your responsibility to see that your phone is answered in a way that is appropriate not only to you, but also to your company. Decide how you want your phones answered and make sure that everyone answers them the same way. One common format is to have the receptionist or whoever answers the phones greet the caller with any one of several salutations ("Hello," "Good morning," "Good afternoon"), followed by the name of the company or organization, the name of the person answering the phone, and finally an offer to help the caller. You may have your staff answer the phones in any professional manner you desire, but generally the more formal, the better. No matter which words are used to greet callers, the person answering the phone should do it in a cheerful, friendly way. The person answering the phone is very important because she represents your company. Often your customer's first impression of your firm is based on their first contact with her. The person answering the phone also can give your callers more personal service by addressing them by their name.

The best way to ensure that your phone is answered the way you want it to be is to answer it yourself. Answering your own phone saves you time in returning phone calls and deciphering messages, and puts you in direct contact with your customers. Your customers and business associates will appreciate the ease with which they can reach you.

Avoid screening your calls if possible. Many people don't like telling others why they're calling to talk to you. If you must have your calls screened, make sure the person doing the screening does so in a professional and courteous way. The person answering the telephone can say, "I'd like to speed up the response from Jeanne. Can I help by getting any documents or items ready for her reference?" Other information that make call screening easier includes a list of people who need to be put in contact with you immediately, such as family members, friends, consultants, and any other important individuals. Clearly specify what you consider to be an emergency and when you want to be interrupted, regardless of whatever else you're doing at the time. Let those answering the telephone know what types of calls they have the authority to handle, what types of calls can be transferred to someone else, and to whom they should be transferred. It's also a good idea to have them keep track of the calls that must be returned that same day.

Transferring calls is an inherent part of telephone etiquette, no matter what your professional position within a company. Whether or not that important customer or client calls back may depend partly on whether she was transferred quickly and accurately to the person she needed to talk to. Being cut off or aimlessly transferred from one department to the next does not impress a business colleague. Don't waste a person's time trying to find the right person. If you don't know, take a message and let the caller know they will receive a return call from the appropriate person. Find out immediately who the appropriate person is and ask them to call back right away. This requires knowing the various departments and who does what in them. Before transferring a call, inform the caller why her call is being transferred and to whom, and assure her that her concern will be successfully addressed. Be sure to include the name, title, division, and extension of the person to whom she is being transferred.

If you must put someone on hold, remember to keep him there no longer than twenty seconds. When circumstances beyond your control make it necessary for the caller to hold for more than twenty seconds, check back with him every thirty to sixty seconds to let him know that you haven't forgotten him. It's also polite to ask if he would prefer calling back later or if you can take a message and have the person get back to him. If another call comes in while you're on another line, put the first person on hold, answer the second call, and put him on hold and then get back to the first caller. Take care of the calls in the order in which they came in. The first caller is dealt with first, the second next, and so on. Only if a call is an emergency, from overseas, or of another particularly unusual nature does it take precedence over any other incoming calls.

Losing a phone number, forgetting a name, and not notifying the manager of an important call are mistakes no one wants to make. A good message is a complete message. It includes the caller's name, telephone number, and phone extension at the name of the company she works for. It should also include the date and time she called and your initials or name, so if there is a question about the message, whoever gets the message will know where to go for more information. Also show on the message whether the person is supposed to return the call and if so, when, or if the caller will call back later.

If you are the caller and must leave a message, leave not only your name, company name and number, but explain briefly why you are calling. This lets the person you were trying reach know why you called and whether he should get back to you immediately. It also enables him to be prepared with documents, information, dates, and other necessary information before calling.

Other thoughts to keep in mind when you're using the telephone:

◄ Try to answer the phone on the first or second ring, and by the fourth ring if at all possible.

◄ Be sure to identify yourself when you answer the phone. It's unreasonable to expect to be recognized by the sound of your voice and inconsiderate to play guessing games with the receptionist.

◄ Make your phone calls directly when possible. Don't waste your secretary's time by asking her to "get someone on the line" for you. If you do have your secretary make the call for you, be on the phone before the person on the other end answers.

◄ If you must cut a call short, offer to call the person back when you can devote more time and your full attention to them. Be sincere and kind. If you choose to tell the caller why you cannot talk just then, use your good business sense. Everyone feels their issue is the most important, so be tactful.

◄ Don't make a phone call unless you have something important to discuss. Needlessly interrupting someone's busy day is inconsiderate. If you have a simple message to leave and don't need to talk with the person, call the secretary directly.

◄ If you want to sound friendly and cheerful over the phone, try smiling and looking up while you're talking! Even though the person on the other end of the phone can't see you, your smile will come through in your voice. You might even try keeping a mirror by the phone as a reminder and to watch yourself as you talk to ensure that you are smiling!

◄ Keep your voice bright and avoid speaking in a monotone. Your interest in your customers comes across clearly over the phone. On the other hand, don't put on an act or exaggerate your inflections.

◄ Avoid making comments such as "I don't know" or "I can't do that," when responding to a caller's request. Rephrase these to sound more accommodating. "Let me see what I can find out" and "I'll see what I can do about that" sound much better. Don't tell the caller you'll be right back unless you know for sure you will be. Ask if you can call back when you find the information.

◄ Pay attention and listen to what your caller is saying. Don't clean your desk, read your mail, or do anything else that would distract you from the conversation you're having.

◄ If you are disconnected when making a call, you—not the party you're calling—are responsible for calling back.

◄ When you have someone in your office, accept only urgent phone calls.

◄ When a client arrives for a scheduled appointment and you are on the phone, end the call quickly and devote your attention to your client.

◄ Take the initiative to leave another person's office if she has a personal emergency or a phone call while you're there. Write a note to have her call you at a certain number, then leave her office. If she says that it's okay for you to stay, don't eavesdrop on the conversation. Look out the window, read something from your briefcase, or devise another means of keeping yourself occupied.

◄ If an associate is on the phone when you arrive at his office, wait outside the door until he is finished unless he motions for you to wait in his office. If you went to his office to notify him of an emergency, it's okay to interrupt his conversation with a note.

◄ If you make a phone call and feel you have been put on "terminal hold," (definitely longer than twenty seconds) hang up and call back, letting the secretary know you were put on hold and then abandoned.

HANDLING CUSTOMER COMPLAINTS

No matter how hard your company tries to keep all its customers satisfied, you're going to get complaints. Unfortunately, most disgruntled customers take it out on the first person they speak to—usually a secretary. It's a shame that anyone has to be exposed to the verbal abuse that often accompanies such calls. To help prevent a confrontation and keep the customer happy, follow these guidelines:

◄ Identify the customer and the complaint.

◄ Ask the complaining customer, "What can we do to make it better?"

◄ Listen and express empathy.

◄ Document the facts—who, what, when, and where. Have the person tell you specifically what happened. Take down the facts, study the situation, and get back to the person as soon as possible. Asking the caller, "May I ask you some specific questions so I get the facts correct?" can make this process easier.

◄ Communicate positively and *avoid reacting defensively*. No one wants to listen to excuses, and no one should have to. Most callers want to know how you will correct the problem.

◄ Restate the problem as you understand it. Repeat the specific facts and details so the customer knows you have the situation correct.

◄ Tell the customer what action you will take and let them know the time frame, and whether you'll get back to them by phone or in writing. Take action as soon as possible. If you feel the need to document your actions, consider a written response .

◄ Express appreciation to the customer for taking time to make the telephone call. Say something to the person like, "Thank you for letting us know so we can take steps to solve this problem." Statements like this go a long way toward getting new business and keeping existing customers happy.

◄ After the call, investigate the customer's complaint and act appropriately. If pertinent, inform the customer in writing of any resolution to the complaint.

AT HOME

If you're like most Americans, you answer your phone by saying "Hello" and then wait for the caller to respond. You end your conversation with "Goodbye." How you say those two words, though, is what matters. Your tone of voice as you answer the phone lets the caller know if he has called you at a good time. If you're curt with your goodbye, your caller may feel as though he was imposing. A person can tell by the sound of your voice whether you're smiling when you're talking on the phone. So if you want to sound more cheerful and enthusiastic on the phone, smile after you dial! As the caller, it's only polite to ask the person you're calling if you've called at a convenient time. Don't assume that just because you have nothing else to do, she doesn't either. As the party being called, it is your responsibility to very politely let the caller know whether you can talk and to find a subtle way to end the conversation if it's getting too long.

Look at the clock before you call. Generally, it's best not to call before 7:00 A.M. or after 10:00 P.M. unless you know that the person you're calling is an early bird or a night owl. Some people prefer that you do not call before 8:00 A.M. or after 9:00 or 9:30 P.M. Definitely do not call someone until late morning on the weekends, and avoid calling at mealtime.

When a member of the household you're calling answers the phone, give your first and last name (skip your title) and the name of the person you'd like to speak with. Don't assume that the person answering the phone will recognize your voice, even if she is the one you want to talk to.

Friends or family members should answer your phone just as they would answer theirs—by saying, "Hello." Only a household employee should answer your phone by saying something such as "the Frederickson home."

How often have you called someone and the first words you heard, in a little child's voice, were "Hi!" or "Who's this?" Children and phones are not really a good combination until children are old enough to answer them and take messages properly. It's up to you to teach your child how you want your phone answered and messages taken. Talking to a child on the phone can be fun if you're his mother, father, grandparent, or another relative, but most people would prefer not have to spend much time talking to your child to get to you.

Limit your conversation to the person on the phone. Don't talk with others in the room, don't have the stereo or TV blaring, and don't eat while you're talking. The telephone magnifies any sounds. Thus, the person on the other end is going to know what you ate for dinner or who your favorite music group is, but she won't know what you said. Remember too, that putting your hand over the receiver when you're talking with someone in the room isn't going to keep everything you say from reaching the person on the other end of the phone. If you don't want that person to hear you, watch what you say or press the mute button.

No matter how good your memory is or how carefully you copied down, you're going to dial a wrong number once in a while. The most courteous way to handle getting a wrong number is to apologize and say that you dialed incorrectly. Simply hanging up without saying anything is very rude and leaves the person on the other end not knowing what to make of the call. It's okay to tell the person the number you were trying to dial or ask her for the number you did reach if you keep reaching her each time you dial. Don't be offended if someone refuses to tell you his number, though. For safety reasons, many choose not to. And, if you're on the receiving end of an incorrectly dialed number, don't feel obligated to give out your telephone number.

VOICE MAIL AND ANSWERING MACHINES

Despite how much you may hate them, you might as well face the fact that answering machines are not going to go away. Although they can be annoying at times, they are convenient. Just think of the messages that would never reach their destinations if it wasn't for voice mail and answering machines. It's best to keep your outgoing message simple, professional, and between 10 and 15 seconds long. You want to include your name, the company you work for, and maybe an estimate of the time you'll be returning. Modify your message to reflect your changing circumstances. On a machine at home, it's best not to include your name or phone number in your message for security reasons. Still, keep your outgoing message between 10 and 15 seconds. Voice-activated message recorders are recommended for both the office and the home because they eliminate the possibility of cutting off a caller who has not finished talking. Many people won't call back to finish their message.

When you leave a message on someone else's answering machine, keep your message to the point. Consider who else might be listening to your message.

When you leave a message on a recorder, give your name, a number where you can be reached or whether you plan to call back later, and a brief explanation of why you're calling. It's thoughtful to include the date and time you called. Don't waste someone else's tape and time by telling them your new joke, filling them in on a new worker in the office, or rambling on about trivia.

SPEAKERPHONES

If you need to bring a number of people together to brainstorm, and you cannot get together physically, speakerphones can be terrific. They are also helpful if you are with a client and need to confer with another professional. For example, you can say, "I have Ms. Jones in my office, and she would like to have your advice. We're on my speakerphone so she can hear your answer."

Whenever you are talking with someone on a speakerphone, let them know they are on a speakerphone. I'll never forget a friend of mind telling me the following story. She had purchased some new business clothing for her sister who was the director of international marketing for a national firm, and she was leaving the following Monday on business travel. My friend had called her sister at work to let her know she had been able to get her some new outfits. When my friend called, her sister was in a meeting with the president, and she was put through to the president's office. My friend had no idea that she was put through to the president's office, and no idea that she was on a speakerphone. She said, "Hi, I have your new clothes." The president's voice then came over the speakerphone and he said, "Hi, tell us all about the new clothes you've gotten your sister." Needless to say, my friend was very embarrassed and quickly let her sister know she would talk with her later.

People who use speakerphones all the time should consider using them in moderation. Many people find speakerphones extremely offensive because they give the impression that you are doing other things while you are talking—which you probably are.

4 High-Tech Etiquette

Fax Finesse

Fax transmission is a commonplace part of business today. Following are some important pointers to ensure your fax communications are making a positive impression for you and your business.

◄ Give your faxes the same professional treatment you do all correspondence.

◄ Send your faxes when promised.

◄ Decide whether or not you need to include a cover sheet stating your name, telephone number, fax number, number of pages, and any other pertinent information. In some cases a cover sheet just adds another unnecessary page to the transmission. In this situation using a small Post-it™ note including your name and telephone number on the first page is all that is necessary. If a cover sheet is used it is counted as page one in the number of pages transmitted.

◄ Sending confidential information via fax can be tricky. Keep in mind that fax correspondence may be read by an entire office before the intended recipient gets it. So anything you don't want others to read should probably not be sent by fax. However, if you do need to fax confidential information, definitely include a cover sheet. Be sure to print or write 'confidential' in large letters across the cover sheet. Also, you want to telephone the recipient before you send the facsimile to arrange if they will be able to be at the machine to receive the transmission when you send it. This will help to ensure confidentiality.

◄ You might want to consider including a confidentiality notice on the facsimile cover page. Companies are including statements such as the following: "The documents accompanying this transmission contain confidential information belonging to the sender which is legally privileged. The information is intended only for the use of the recipient named above. If you are not the privileged recipient, beware that any disclosure, copying, distribution or use of the contents of this telecopied information is prohibited. If you have received the telecopy in error, please immediately notify the sender."

◄ You may want to notify the recipient by phone that the fax has been sent. This follow-up is recommended particularly in large businesses and corporations, where a transmission can easily get lost, mistakenly clipped to a previous fax, or routed to the wrong person or department. The intended recipient may finally get the fax hours later or not at all. In either case, your credibility suffers.

◄ Keep the receipt of each fax transmission. This goes without saying in case you need to verify to your client when your fax transmission was sent.

◄ Unless you've been requested to do so, be sensitive about sending more than three or four pages via fax. When a fax line is also the person's or company's telephone line this consideration is appreciated. If you do need to transmit a long document, try to send it at a time of day that the fax machine may be less busy.

◄ Make a photocopy of any document on colored or textured papers. Colored paper slows down the fax transmission, making the procedure costlier and more time-consuming. Textured paper can appear with the texture printed in black all over the document making it difficult to read and appearing immensely sloppy, as well as making the fax transmission slower and costlier.

◄ If you've used correction fluid on your document, be sure to fax a photocopy rather than the original. Correction fluid appears as a blotch when faxed. Also, pencil marks and light blue ink do not transmit well.

◄ Any unsolicited fax should be no more than a single page.

◄ Sign your fax messages for a more personal touch.

ELECTRONIC MAIL (E-MAIL) ETIQUETTE

Who could have envisioned, just a few years ago, that e-mail would allow us, at the push of a button, to send messages immediately all over the world? In 1993 an estimated 25 million e-mailboxes existed in the U.S., and 12.5 million were reported in Europe. E-mail messaging is one of the most exciting aspects of the Internet. You can contact friends and colleagues around the globe no matter who they have as their Internet service provider. The Internet thus becomes a common carrier of information, a shared link between people to access its resources.

This late-20th-century electronic correspondence now gives the etiquette mavens one more thing to debate. Some etiquette experts are holding their ground and saying that electronic mail is okay for business, but for a social letter, paper is still proper. It may amuse you to know that there were raging debates during the last century about whether it was impolite to send personal correspondence by mail! It was thought to be so impersonal. And one of the objections raised was that people would not answer invitations immediately, as they had to when the footman stood his ground until given a response. Just as we had to accept invitations by post we need to quickly accept social correspondence by e-mail. Business associates and family members all over the world are keeping in touch more than ever because of the ease of e-mail. While this new technology can expedite the transmission of information, it can also sour your relationship with others as quickly as you push that computer key. Remember to only write those things you would tell someone if you were talking to them.

The content and maintenance of a user's electronic mailbox is the users responsibility. Be sure to check e-mail daily and remain within your limited disk quota. Delete unwanted messages immediately since they take up disk storage. Keep messages remaining in your electronic mailbox to a minimum. Messages can be downloaded or extracted to files, then to disks for future reference. Following are two other important pointers.

There are two things that stand out in business professionals minds regarding e-mail etiquette. The first is that you should not write a message in all capitals because that comes across as screaming or shouting at a person. Or, as if you're wanting some kind of attention immediately...right away. It feels very demanding. What you want to do is write your e-mail message as you would write a letter. Capitalize words only to highlight an important point or to distinguish a title or heading. *Asterisks* surrounding a word also can be used to make a stronger point. Format your messages so they look like a memo or a letter. Use complete sentences. Remember this form of electronic transmission is just replacing the paper. The speed of the technology doesn't give you a license to be sloppy. When replying to e-mail include as much of the original message as necessary to set the context of your reply.

The second important point business professionals mention is that the name of the person you are addressing the e-mail to should always be in upper case. Many systems have a very helpful feature that will automatically put the person you are addressing your e-mail to in upper case, even if you cntcrcd it in lower case.

If you receive an e-mail message that appears to have some unknown acronyms and strange computer gibberish made up of commas, colons and every imaginable keyboard character, tilt your head 90 degrees to your left shoulder. At that angle you usually can see faces emerge from the gibberish, such as a smiley face made up of colon, dash and parenthesis, like :-). These are "emoticons,"—the merging of the words "emotion" and "lexicon"—are little face images made up of characters on your keyboard that help give context and nuance to what you write. It's the equivalent of smiling or winking at a person as you talk. In cyberspace it's a way of trying to avoid misunderstandings when you are communicating with people who can't see you and often don't know you. Emoticons have sprung up because e-mail is single dimension communication. To help convey meaning learn some common emoticons like :-(I'm sad; ;-) I'm winking-sarcasm; :-D I'm laughing; :'-(I'm crying; :-# My lips are sealed; :-J I'm being tongue-in-cheek; :-I I'm indifferent; :-/ I'm perplexed; :-O I'm surprised; :-& I'm tongue-tied; and :-> I'm grinning.

Include your signature at the bottom of e-mail messages. Your signature footer should include your name, position, affiliation and Internet address, and should not exceed more than 4 lines. Optional information could include your address and phone number.

A useful feature of e-mail is that you can use it to sign up for mailing lists—electronic discussion areas where people exchange messages on a whole library of topics. Check the Internet Resources Forum's Library 8, "Mailing Lists," to get samples of mailing lists you might like to subscribe to. All messages posted to the group's central address are distributed to the mailboxes of subscribers, each of whom has the opportunity to answer them. To join a mailing list, send mail to the appropriate address. In the message, simply ask to be added to the subscription list, and postings will soon begin to arrive in your mailbox. If you subscribe to mailing lists, be advised that some of them carry heavy traffic. Internet access providers usually charge members a small fee per message, a fee that is offset by the monthly usage allowance. While there is no charge if you delete a message without reading it, you should keep this charge in mind with any incoming Internet mail. When signing up for a group it is important to save your subscription confirmation letter for reference. That way when you go away for more than a week, you will have the subscription address for unsubscribing or suspending mail from the mailing lists.

INTERNET "CULTURE" OR "NETIQUETTE"

The Internet is the worldwide matrix of connecting computers using the Transmission Control (TCP) and Internet (IP) protocols. The Transmission Control Protocol is the set of protocols that determine how data is transmitted on the Internet. TCP controls the transport of data, ensuring that it is delivered. IP determines the packet structure of data and the addressing used to deliver data to its destination. The World Wide Web is a system that organizes Internet data through hypertext links, allowing you to explore resources from multiple entry points using a browser. "netiquette" is the etiquette of using the Internet; it's the way the Internet community describes politeness when using newsgroups, and other forms of communicating, like e-mail.

Since this is such a new technology connecting networks are developing their policies as they are needed. There are rapidly developing do's and don'ts. One big don't is, don't do unsolicited mailing! You can of course have a homepage and advertise various pieces of information. Individuals are able to request the information they want.

Here are some additional tips to help ensure that your cyberspace communications are working to project the image you want.

◄ Don't forget that at the other end of your note will be a real live person. When you are sitting alone at your computer, writing to a discussion group may give the impression of anonymity, however it may be one of the most public things you ever do. When you communicate electronically, all you see is a computer screen. As you write, imagine how you'd feel if you were in the other person's shoes. Stand up for yourself, but try not to hurt people's feelings. When you're holding a conversation on-line, whether it's an e-mail exchange or a response to a discussion group posting, it's easy to have your meaning or your correspondent's meaning misinterpreted.

◄ When you communicate through cyberspace, via e-mail or on discussion groups, your words are written and may be stored or forwarded somewhere. In other words, there's a good chance they can come back to haunt you. You have no control over where it goes. You may want to ask yourself the following question, "Would I be willing to appear on the evening news tonight making this statement?" It might help you keep the perspective and reputation you really want—and, save you from cyberspace embarrassment.

◄ Adhere to the same standards of behavior online that you use with personal contacts. Don't violate laws of libel, defamation, copyright, or any other laws. Use the same standard of ethics and behavior in cyberspace that you use with personal contacts.

◄ Know where you are in cyberspace. Internet culture or "netiquette" is not the same in every domain. What may be perfectly acceptable in one area may be dreadfully rude in another. When you enter a domain of cyberspace that's new to you, take some time to look around. Spend a while listening to the chat or reading the archives to get a sense of how the people who are already there act.

◄ Respect other people's time to ensure the time they spend reading your posting isn't wasted. Be descriptive in subject headings. The headline is the first thing people will use to decide whether or not to read your article. When you post the same note to the same newsgroup several times, you are wasting the time of individuals who are checking the multiple postings. If you're new and trying to see if you know how to send a posting, don't send 'Only Testing' posts to newsgroups other than alt.newusers or misc. tst. It's rude and wastes time and space.

◄ Help others when they have questions about things you know. Share expert knowledge. The strength of cyberspace is in its numbers. The reason asking questions online works is that a lot of knowledgeable people are reading the questions. Be sure to check Frequently Asked Questions (FAQ) for the Newsgroup or alt.newusers.questions for common questions and answers before you ask a question. You may find your questions already have been answered.

◄ The Internet was founded and grew because scientists wanted to share information. Don't be afraid to share what you know. It's especially polite to share the results of your questions with others. If you anticipate that you'll get a lot of answers to a question, or when you post a question to a discussion group that you don't visit often, it's customary to request replies by e-mail instead of to the group. After you get all the responses, write up a summary and post it to the discussion group. That way everyone benefits from the expertise of those who took the time to answer you. Sharing your knowledge is fun.

◄ Assist in keeping flame wars under control. "Flaming" is the term used for uncivilized behavior on the Internet. With over 9,000 discussion groups on the Internet, just about every topic imaginable (or absolutely unimaginable) is discussed. These discussions sometimes provide more heat than light. Something about the nature of the network communications seems to lead some people to lose perspective and respond in overly harsh ways. These negative comments and reactions are called "flames" or "flaming" on the Internet. Some who have strong opinions but have retained perspective will, in jest, write "set flame on," then proceed to have their say, followed by the words "set flame off," just to let you know that they feel strongly about the subject, but are still open to reason. It is good for the newcomer to be aware of flaming so as not to take it too seriously—and end up responding with flames.

◄ Respect other people's privacy. You'd never dream of going through a colleagues desk drawer, so don't read their e-mail either. Failing to respect other people's privacy is not just bad "netiquette." It has cost some people their jobs.

◄ Keep in mind that some discussion groups have members from many countries. You may need to be more descriptive of "local" references.

◄ Be forgiving of other people's mistakes on the Internet. Everyone was a cyberspace "newbie" once. If it's a minor error, you may not need to say anything. If you do decide to inform someone of a mistake, point it out in a friendly and supportive way; preferably by private e-mail rather than in public.

BEEPERS (PAGING EQUIPMENT)

Beepers are important in our fast-paced business world. Still, they can be a disturbance in meetings. One department manager of a firm remarked that in a meeting attended by twenty people, beepers were sounding constantly. The noise clearly disrupted the speaker as well as the participants in the meeting. In fact, the department manager remarked that what really bothered her was not only that the beeper went off, but more noticeably that the person did not even leave the room to return what would appear to be an important call. Thus, it appeared that the meeting was disrupted for something that was not important. Today's beepers come with a variety of alert options - a light, a tone or a silent vibration. If it is critical that you be contacted during a meeting, prior to entering switch your beeper to the soundless vibrating mode, so you can feel the alert, but no one else in the room will hear it, or just leave it off and check for messages during breaks.

When attending a meeting or a public performance you may want to use the silent vibration alert which gives you voice mail, numeric or alpha messages.

If your beeper goes off during a business meeting, and the message requires an urgent response, then excuse yourself and leave. With a numeric beeper, you can design special codes so you know when you have received an urgent message. With an alphanumeric beeper you can see the full message and know if it is an emergency call.

In today's paging equipment market, the silent alert features along with numeric and alpha messaging make communication easily accessible. You can be reached and no one else in the room is disturbed by your customers paging you with their messages. Even so, it is important to remember to use beepers judiciously, courteously and professionally.

CELLULAR (PORTABLE, MOBILE, OR TRANSPORTABLE) TELEPHONES

Like beepers, cellular telephones brought to a meeting are distracting to participants and speaker. Again, unless it is critical that you be contacted directly during the meeting leave your cellular phone back at the office, or in your car. The main point is courtesy to all participants at a meeting.

The advancement of cellular technology has meant that people are now able to talk on the phone anywhere: on street corners, in restaurants, at airports, almost everywhere. The freedom and flexibility that cellular phones afford is a most productive advancement. Used wisely, cellular phones can make our work easier and faster. Remember the following guidelines wherever and whenever you use a cellular phone:

◀ Bringing a cellular phone to a public place, such as a restaurant, should be done only when absolutely necessary. Ask others present if they mind if you use your phone while you are with them. When on a lengthy call, excuse yourself and complete the conversation elsewhere.

◀ Due to the large number of cellular phones, numerous restaurants, particularly upscale restaurants do not allow them. They feel they are perceived as an intrusion to other people. So, if you do bring your cellular phone with you into a restaurant, you will want to check with the maitre d', or your server, to be sure it is even allowed.

◀ If you are in your office and place a call to someone using a car phone, remember talking and driving can be difficult and hazardous. The driver may not be able to stop and and write down information. If you are using a car phone, be sure to alert the person you are talking to that there is a chance you may drive out of the cellular coverage area or encounter interference and if this happens that you will call them back as soon as possible.

◀ If you know you will be conducting a lot of business while driving, a speaker phone in your car is a good option as it allows you to keep both hands on the wheel. Whether in your office or car, always advise the caller you are using a speaker phone if others are present with you.

TELECONFERENCING/VIDEOCONFERENCING

Many businesses today bring together groups of people to save time, money and energy regardless of location by means of teleconferencing/videoconferencing. It is said that in the U.S. there are 20 million business meetings held each day. Executives devote up to 46% of their time in meetings, with 75% of that time used traveling to and from the meetings.

For a scheduled teleconference consider these suggestions:

◄ Be sure everyone knows why the teleconference has been scheduled, and what is supposed to be accomplished. This allows participants to come prepared and to stay focused on the topic. Teleconferences still take people away from other work, even though they aren't spending time traveling.

◄ Develop a time table and an agenda. Send or fax it to the participants well in advance of the teleconference. Teleconferences usually cover items more quickly than face-to-face meetings.

◄ Have participants RSVP. This way you will know how large a room is necessary for the teleconference.

◄ At the beginning give everyone the ground rules for the teleconference. Ask them to wait to comment until the current speaker is finished talking. Also, ask them not to interrupt a person who is speaking. Provide them with any other applicable ground rules for your particular teleconference

◄ Ask participants to identify themselves at the beginning of the teleconference so each voice will be recognizable, and perhaps repeat this if the teleconference is lengthy.

◄ Ask participants to speak clearly and distinctly at a volume that is comfortable for the other participants.

◄ Be sure the teleconferencing/videoconferencing equipment (speaker phones, video units, etc.) and the room you are using are of high quality to eliminate echos, distortion, clipped words, muddied voices and background noises.

5 Introductions

No matter how you goof up while making introductions—whether you forget Mrs. Diddlebacher's name, introduce Mr. Harris to a person he already knows, present Mrs. Cooper's husband as her father, or make any other of the infinite possibilities for error—what's important is that you attempted the introduction. Almost any error you make while introducing someone will be graciously forgiven. What may not be so easily forgiven, is neglecting to introduce someone at all. It's most inconsiderate to ignore someone or to avoid introducing someone to others. Like the information on handshakes, this chapter on Introductions is one of the most sought after and used references by business people. Since introductions are everyday occurrences in business, it's important to know the basic rules. While the following guidelines probably won't help you remember a person's name, who's related to whom, or what someone's occupation is, they will help you ease some of your fears about making proper introductions. To remember a person's name, listen carefully to the name and look at the person you are being introduced to.

THE BASIC INTRODUCTION

Probably the easiest introduction to make is introducing one person to another. The basic rule for making this type of introduction is to remember introductions are based on rank. The person in the higher ranking position is mentioned first. Clients, senior executives, or distinguished guests can be considered authority figures, or persons of importance. You introduce people to them. Always try to remember the star gets top billing, thus they're mentioned first. Following are some helpful introduction fundamentals.

◄ A younger person is typically introduced to an older person. Say the older persons name first. "Mr. Parker, this is Tim Jones. Tim, this is Mr. Parker, my Dad."

◄ A nonofficial or nondignitary is typically presented to an official or dignitary.

◄ A peer in your company is introduced to a peer from another company, and an executive is introduced to a customer or client. "Bob Smith (your client), this is Doug Johnson, (your boss), senior vice president of Raytech Industries. Doug, this is Bob Smith, marketing director of Sunray Incorporated." Whether they are a man or a woman, the customer's name should always be said first. Traditionally business introductions are based on rank rather than gender.

◄ Always introduce your spouse to your boss. The bosses name is said first. "Mr. Brodersen, I'd like you to meet my husband, Phil Parker. Phil, this is Mr. Brodersen, my boss."

◄ Here's a sticky one over which many have agonized: How does one introduce a live-in partner? Very simply. If you are introducing your live-in, Steve, to your boss, simply say, "Paul Williams, I'd like you to meet Steve Carlson. Steve, I'd like you to meet Paul Williams, my boss." Nothing more needs to be said.

◄ If you and your spouse do not have the same last name, take great pains to introduce your spouse with the correct last name. If a David Olson were to introduce his wife to a colleague, he would say, "Tom Smith, this is my wife, Susan Harris. Susan, this is Tom Smith."

◄ Junior executives are presented to senior executives. Again, it's traditional in introduction etiquette to have company hierarchy dictate who is introduced to whom. "Ms. Thomas (senior executive) I'd like you to meet our marketing assistant, Bob Jones. Bob, this is Ms. Thomas, our CEO."

◄ All guests, unless they are dignitaries or elderly, are introduced to the guest of honor.

The most standard and accepted responses to an introduction are "How do you do" and "I'm pleased to meet you." Inappropriate responses are "I'm glad to know you," "Charmed," "Pleased," or "Pleased to know you." You can't say with sincerity that you are glad or pleased to know someone when you've just been introduced and really don't know him.

When you meet someone for the first time, stand while being introduced to her. Always rise. Not only is standing more attractive than sitting, but it also shows respect. Only if you are elderly, ill, or physically unable to stand is it acceptable for you to remain seated while greeting your guests or being introduced.

When you take the initiative and introduce yourself to someone you don't know, give your first and last names, "Hello, I'm David Miller."

When introducing two people, include some information about each of them. You could say something like, "Ms. Winters, I'd like you to meet my business partner, Ms. Susan Taylor. Susan, this is Ms. Cindy Winters. Cindy recently started a business similar to ours." Including extra information, such as their occupation, who their family is, or how you know each other provides a base from which two people can start a conversation. If the gathering is a business function, the information you include is usually something you know the other two will have in common, an occupational title, or something else that is work related. Chances are, the conversation will proceed on its own after that.

Always make sure everyone knows one another. An attorney tells about a situation where she had recently been elected to a new Board of Directors position for a non-profit association along with two other people. The new Board members attended the first meeting, of course expecting to be introduced at some point. She couldn't believe it when she and the other new Board appointees went home not having been introduced to anyone the whole evening. If she had known this would be the case she would have taken an opportunity and introduced herself at some appropriate point in the meeting, or mentioned it to the chairperson during break so the introductions could have been made thereafter. This example once again serves as a reminder that even top level executives can forget to make introductions.

Don't worry about making mistakes when introducing people to one another; the most important thing is to make the introduction. Ask two people: "Do you know each other?" If they don't, let them introduce themselves to one another, and then you don't have to worry about making any mistakes. This also works well when you can't remember the name of one of the people or where they work. Another thing you can do is say the name of the person you know and hope the other person will introduce herself.

Often it is difficult to remember people's names until we know something about them. You will increase the chance of having your name remembered if you first give some information about yourself and then say your name.

If you are a tax accountant, you could say something like, "You know what April 15th means. Yes, I am a tax accountant." Then, state your name and end by expressing interest in getting to know the other person. For example, you could say: "I'm looking forward to getting to know you." Take a few moments now to create an interesting introduction for yourself. You want to keep it short and to the point, but any humor or interesting piece of information you can add will help people remember your name. And that is the name of the game—getting people to remember you.

GROUP INTRODUCTIONS

If you are giving or attending a party and are the only one who knows a new member or particular guest, take it upon yourself to introduce him to the rest of the group. Unless the group is somewhat small—perhaps five or six people—don't bother introducing him to everyone at once; that is too many names for anyone to remember.

Just introduce him to the two or three people who are standing or sitting closest to him. You'll most likely find that others will start introducing themselves, and the rest of the introductions will take care of themselves. Remember to provide some information about the person when you introduce him. Any time you are at a social gathering and the host doesn't introduce you to the other guests, it is acceptable for you to introduce yourself.

To introduce a client to a group of people, say, "Mr. Client, may I present the members of our sales staff." When you introduce a new colleague to the group, the order changes: "Ladies and gentlemen, I'd like you to meet our new colleague, Mr. Green." Even better would be to act as escort and introduce the new person to each individual in the group.

When a group of business women were asked in a recent study how they would most like to be addressed, rather than "ladies," or "female," most preferred the term "women."

For a recent meeting, a project manager, prepared name tags for everyone attending. Name tags prepared in advance are always welcome, as they immediately tell guests, "We were expecting you." This time the project manager put everyone's name on the top half of the name tag and left space at the bottom. As they arrived, he asked people to add something to their name tag as a conversation starter. Some people put a question, statement, picture, or name of an activity they enjoyed. This turned out to be a terrific networking activity and helped everyone easily start conversations with others in the group. It was interesting to see how the information they provided immediately gave additional insight into their personalities. And it was often information that would not have been provided if people were simply introduced. For example, one person wrote, "You talk, I'll listen." Another wrote, "Ask me about traveling." and someone else said, "Swimming with six dolphins."

There are times when introductions may not be necessary. If you're walking with a group and happen to meet someone you know, you're not required to introduce this person to your colleagues. If you stop to chat, tell the group to go ahead and you'll catch up with them. If you are dining with a group and someone you know happens to walk by your table, you're not obligated to introduce that person to the other diners. If you wish to have a brief conversation, step away from the table.

TITLES

Unless the person you're introducing is older than you, is a professional, or has an official ranking, don't use her title when introducing her. Do include a former officials title when introducing her, even when she no longer holds the position. For example, you'd introduce a former Congressperson as "former U.S. Representative Julie Brown" or "former member of Congress Julie Brown."

When introducing a widow, it is thoughtful to mention her husband's name also. For example, "Sara Winters, I'd like you to meet Ted Sampson, my business associate. Ted, this is Sara Winters. Her late husband, Brad, and I went to college together."

It is never appropriate for people to introduce themselves and include the forms of "Ms.," "Mrs.," or "Mr." in their names.

WHEN YOU FORGET A NAME

"I'd like to introduce . . . ahh, umm . . . I'm sorry, what was your name again?" How often has each of us forgotten the name of a person we were supposed to introduce? I don't think there is anyone who always remembers everyone's name. If you do forget someone's name when introducing him, it's perfectly okay to admit that you have forgotten it. It's better to have him say it than for you to call him by another name or neglect to introduce him at all. Be calm and straightforward and say something like, "I remember meeting you, but I simply cannot recall your name." Or, "I'm having trouble recalling your name." Some people use computer terminology: "I was positive I'd stored your name in my memory, but I'm obviously having difficulty retrieving it." This is a subtle, amusing way of reminding people we are human, after all, and allowed to make mistakes.

If your friend, or anyone else for that matter, forgets your name while introducing you, don't just stand there and laugh while she struggles with her momentary memory lapse. Immediately help her out by saying your name and extending your hand for a handshake. The person you're meeting will do the same. Always introduce yourself by using your first and last name, but never include your title.

INTRODUCING COMPANIONS

When you and a companion are walking down the street or shopping in the supermarket and you run into an old acquaintance, whether to introduce your companion to your acquaintance is a judgment call on your part. If the conversation will be short and trivial— such as "Hi, how are you doing? I haven't seen you in a long time"— there is probably no need for everyone to be formally introduced. If however, you feel your companion and acquaintance might have something in common or would benefit from knowing one another, introduce them. Apply the same reasoning when deciding whether to introduce yourself to your acquaintance's companion.

If your companion happens to be your spouse, she typically is introduced. The only situations in which it's alright for you not to introduce her is when the encounter is brief and she is not likely to again see the person. You can still say, "I'd like you to meet my spouse," and hope the other person will volunteer and introduce themselves. If you happen to meet a business associate or friend and your children are with you, always introduce your children. Teach them to voluntarily shake hands when introduced.

There is no need for you to introduce a household worker, such as a nanny or a gardener, to your guests. But if you feel comfortable introducing them, by all means do so. If you have a secretary and you have him come into a meeting to take minutes or to bring in refreshments, it is a courteous acknowledgment to introduce him.

EXAMPLES

Although there is not one correct way to word an introduction, the most common are, "I'd like you to meet . . ." and "I'd like to introduce . . ." Remember to use always first and last names when introducing people. The "Don, this is Nancy. Nancy, this is Don" method is unacceptable, as it implies that you don't trust one or both of the people enough to use their full names. When you are unsure, it's always better to make your introductions more conservative than not, and to use titles and surnames—"Peg, I'd like you to meet my colleague from XYZ Corporation, Kathy Smith. Kathy, this is my friend, Mrs. Peg Jackson."

6 Invitations Made Easy

Business events are designed not only to let you schmooze with your favorite client at your function, but also to allow you to increase company visibility with all your business contacts. Increasing visibility is a good idea: Your company receives extra publicity, you have a chance to make more contacts in your industry, and your company can make more money by the increased exposure.

BUSINESS INVITATIONS

Business invitations can be informal or formal. Business invitations are usually sent through the mail, but informal invitations such as letters, Mailgrams, and phone invitations are becoming more acceptable. For most informal occasions, it's best to invite guests three to four weeks in advance. If you choose to invite your guests by phone, remind them again in writing two weeks before the gathering. This gives both of you enough time. It gives you enough time to add and delete guests from your list. It gives the guest enough time to decide whether to accept or decline your invitation. One helpful hint: If you send 200 invitations, you can expect about 40 people to show up. This is a good guideline when trying to predict how many people you will have at your party.

Formal business invitations are most commonly engraved or printed in black, navy, dark gray, or brown ink on white or off-white high-quality paper. A company can use any color of paper it desires, as long as it upholds and promotes the company's image.

On the business invitation, you will find (1) the company logo or symbol, (2) the names of the host, (3) the invitation phrase, (4) the nature of the party, (5) the purpose of the party, (6) the date, (7) the time, (8) the place, (9) where to RSVP, and (10) any special instructions. You will usually find the company logo on the top or bottom of the invitation. If the company name is included in the logo, it need not be mentioned again in the body of the invitation. It may be included in the RSVP information with the company's address, ZIP code, and telephone number.

Formal and business invitations:

1. Corporate logo and name
(logo also may be at the bottom)

2. Mr. James Wilson, Vice President of XYZ Corporation
and the Honorable Pat Wilson

3. cordially invite you to

4. Dinner

5. to celebrate
the Corporation's 25-year anniversary

6. Saturday, the twenty-fifth of August

7. at six-thirty o'clock

8. The Boulder Inn
Address

9. RSVP   10. Black Tie
Ms. Pat Wilson
Address
Telephone Number

It's not enough to have on the invitation just the name of the company that is sponsoring the party or dinner. The names of the people giving the event—even if it's a broad title such as the board of directors—need to be included. When there is only one host, list the name of the company above the name of that person. Include that person's title.

When there is one host:

> SUPERIOR SERVICES CORPORATION
> Janice Thompson, Regional Manager,
> requests your presence at

If a group is giving the event, such as a board or company department, list the title of that group above the name of the company.

When a group is hosting:

> The Marketing and Sales Departments
> of the SUPERIOR SERVICES CORPORATION
> cordially invite you to

If the event is given by two people, list the name of the company before the the names and titles of the people. You may list the names, according to professional position, either horizontally or vertically.

When there are two hosts:

> SUPERIOR SERVICES CORPORATION
> Mary Johnson, Marketing Manager
> James Wilson, Sales Manager
> request your presence at

> or

> SUPERIOR SERVICES CORPORATION
> Mary Johnson, Marketing Manager
> James Wilson, Sales Manager
> cordially invite you to

Three hosts can be listed, according to professional position, either vertically or in a triangle.

When there are three hosts:

SUPERIOR SERVICES CORPORATION
Mary Johnson, Marketing Manager James Wilson, Sales Manager
Karen Young, Advertising Executive
request your presence at

or

SUPERIOR SERVICES CORPORATION
Mary Johnson, Marketing Manager
James Wilson, Sales Manager
Karen Young, Advertising Executive
cordially invite you to

If there are many hosts and they all have about the same professional position, list them alphabetically. If one of them has a title, a title must be used with the name of each host. If the name of the company isn't included in the logo or symbol, list it after the host's title.

When there are many hosts:

THE ADVERTISING ALLIANCE

Elizabeth Anderson, Anderson Advertising
Robert Chandler, R. C. Advertising
Jane Paulson, Amazing Ads
Ted Simpson, Simpson and Associates Advertising
cordially invite you to

To list an executive and a spouse as the hosts, list the name and title of the executive first, followed by the name and title of the spouse (for example, Mr., Mrs., the Honorable).

When an executive and their spouse host:

Mr. John Anderson, President of Medical Research, Inc.
and Mrs. Anderson
request your presence at

Mrs. Katherine Lawson, chairperson of Temps, Inc.
and Mr. Tom Lawson
request your presence at

The Doctors Johnson
cordially invite you to

If they're both executives and play an equal role in giving the event, and the wife is an official, such as a judge, member of Congress or city council member, she is listed first as "The Honorable" followed by her name. If the husband is hosting and the wife is at the party but not as the host, his name is listed first.

When an executive and his wife host and she is an official:

> The Honorable Nancy Sims and Mr. Tyler Sims
> cordially invite you to . . .

When he is the host and she is an official:

> Mr. Tyler Sims and the Honorable Nancy Sims
> cordially invite you to . . .

PARTS OF AN INVITATION

The invitation phrase is nothing more than the line that says something such as "you are cordially invited to" or "requests the pleasure of your company at." Some others are "requests your presence at," "invites you to," and "requests the honor of your presence." The phrase you use depends upon your company, the occasion, and how formal you want to be.

The type and purpose of the party are just that. State whether the event is for breakfast, luncheon, or dinner, a cocktail party or some other occasion to introduce someone or a new product, to honor a retiree, or to celebrate an occasion or another festive event.

The most formal invitations have the date and time of the event completely written out. Never abbreviate days of the week. The most formal style is to write, "Friday, the twenty-seventh of July at six-thirty o'clock." The least formal is "Friday, July 27, at 6:00 P.M."

The address where the event will be held is next. A map is typically included with the invitation if your house or the country club is difficult to find or if your guests haven't been there before. The RSVP address or phone number is in the bottom left-hand corner of the invitation, and across from that are any special instructions such as attire, parking instructions, where the event will be held in case of rain, and so on.

Preprinted invitations work well for most informal dinners and parties. For a casual gathering, there is no need to have invitations printed or engraved or to spend much money on them. Preprinted invitations work well and can be fun. They're convenient, come in a variety of shapes, sizes, and colors, and are available for almost every occasion. They range from very informal to formal. To personalize your informal invitations even more, you may want to use your stationery.

With preprinted invitations, you simply fill the blanks, in neat handwriting, to tell what, where, and when the party will be and who is giving it. When using your stationery, you can follow this same format, or you may want to write a note to the person you're inviting that includes this information. It's also acceptable to include an RSVP notation and your phone number or address on the invitation. One events planner believes every invitation should include an RSVP response. Why? For more accurate planning.

Informal preprinted invitation:

We hope you can attend!

Event: _____

When: _____

Where: _____

Host: _____

Informal short note on your stationery:

Dear Doug and Nancy,

Jay and I are planning a Labor Day barbeque at our home at 1:00 P.M. We hope you and your family can come. Please call and let us know if you will be able to come. We look forward to seeing you soon.

Warm regards,

Mary

RESPONDING

You may be asked to respond to an invitation in a variety of ways. One common way is to use the address or phone number printed in the lower left corner of the invitation. Another is to return the RSVP card sent with the invitation. This is perhaps the most convenient way for the invited person to respond. If a phrase such as "Please reply by" a given date is included in the invitation, be considerate enough to reply by that date. If the words "Regrets only" are printed in the lower left corner of the invitation, you need only notify the host if you will not be able to attend. If your host does not hear from you, you are expected to attend.

Just as there are many ways that you can be asked to respond, there are a variety of ways in which you can notify the host whether you will be attending. The easiest is to return the RSVP card sent with the invitation. A quicker way is to telephone the person's office. You also could send a typed or handwritten formal reply or personal note. If you do this, however, don't reply on any piece of paper; be sure to use high-quality stationery. Finally, you could send a Mailgram. If you are away on an extended business trip, your secretary may respond for you, either by returning the RSVP card or sending a short note.

Formal acceptance:

Mr. Andrew Fredericks
accepts with pleasure
Mr. and Mrs. James Wilson's invitation
to dinner on
Friday, the twenty-fifth of August
at six-thirty o'clock
at The Boulder Inn

Formal regrets:

Mr. Andrew Fredericks
sincerely regrets
that he will be unable to accept
Mr. and Mrs. James Wilson's invitation
to dinner
Friday, the twenty-fifth of August

Your host may have subtly suggested that you may bring someone with you by including a guest line on the RSVP card. If such a line is present, you may fill in your guest's name and business affiliation. A guest line doesn't mean that you are obligated to bring someone else. You may, of course, bring a guest if your envelope is addressed to you and "guest" or if your host otherwise suggests that it's okay for you to do so.

If you invite others to an informal event in person or over the phone, don't expect them to be able to give you an answer right away. They may need to check with their spouse or consult their calendar before they're able to give you an answer. Those invited need to accept or decline as soon as possible and not wait until the day before or the day of the event to let the host know whether they will be attending. It's better to be sooner than later. And, it is unacceptable to simply show up without replying at all. When a couple has been invited and only one person can attend, that person should decline. They should let the host know they declined because their partner could not attend. This gives the host the option of offering to invite the couple to their next dinner party or letting the one person who is able to come know that he or she is still welcome.

One should never ask for permission to bring a guest unless the invitation states "Mr. James Brown and Guest," or as mentioned if there is a line on the RSVP card where you can write your guest's name. Showing up with an uninvited friend could turn out to be an embarrassing situation for everyone. If you don't want to go to the party or dinner without that special someone, decline the invitation. Let the host know that you'd like to get together with him at a time when your friend can accompany you.

If you'll be having out-of-town guests at your home the same night as a party you've been invited to, let your host know that you'll be unable to attend. Be careful not to make him feel guilty or as if he needs to extend the invitation to your guests. In this situation, you can say something like, "We'd love to come, but some out-of-town friends are visiting that night, and we're going to catch up on lost time with them. Sorry we can't make it, but let's get together another time."

REMINDER CARDS

Reminder cards are used for business and formal events and also for informal events. You may send (or receive) a reminder card when invitations are given in person or over the phone. Sending a card in this instance is very important because it is most likely the only written record of the date, time, and place of the event. If a company sends invitations to an important event many months in advance, it's a good idea to send a reminder card ten days to two weeks before the event to refresh people's memories. If the time or location of an event must be changed after invitations have been sent, especially if they've been sent well in advance, a reminder card informs guests of the change of time or location.

The information in a business or formal reminder card is essentially the same as that in an informal reminder card. It states that it is a reminder that you (the guest) are expected at (type of event) on (date) at (time). Also included are the name and address of the company or person giving the event or the address of the location of the event, if it's different, and possibly a reminder of the attire expected or other special instructions.

After inviting someone by phone, send a reminder card no later than two weeks before the event. A reminder card can be anything— a postcard, a sheet of your personal stationery, or an informal or preprinted invitation. The message can be very simple: "This is a reminder that (host's name) is looking forward to seeing you for (name of occasion) on (date) at (time)." Any similar message is fine. Also include your address. Don't expect a reply from reminder cards unless something comes up and a guest who previously accepted your invitation is no longer able to come.

Informal reminder card:
This is to remind you that
Jim and Pat Wilson
are looking forward to seeing you
for:
on:
at:

Formal reminder card:

Corporate name
Address

Host's name   Date
Title

To remind you of
a luncheon
Honoring Carolyn Smith's promotion
Thursday, the sixteenth of June
at eleven-thirty o'clock
The Riverside Inn
Address
Host's telephone number

Just how far in advance should you mail invitations? That depends upon the particular event you're giving, but the sooner you send out your invitation, the sooner your guests can mark it on their calendars and plan to attend before something else is planned for that time. Here are some general time lines to follow:

◄ Six to eight months before an important seminar to which out-of-town executives are invited.

◄ Four to six months before an important dinner to which out-of-town guests are invited.

◄ Three to five weeks before a luncheon.

◄ Four weeks before an evening reception.

◄ Two to four weeks before a breakfast for a large group.

◄ Two to four weeks before a cocktail party.

◄ Two to three weeks before a tea party.

CANCELED EVENT

If the date of the event should happen to change or the event must be canceled altogether after the invitations have been sent and the guests have responded, notify all guests immediately if the date of the event is near. The quickest way is to notify them by phone, or by Mailgram if they're out of town. Also let the guests know why the date has been changed or the event canceled. If you send out a second set of invitations after changing the date, be sure to include not only the new date, but also the date the event was previously planned for and invite those who declined the first invitation. If you change the date of or cancel an event but still have a good deal of time before the date for which the event was previously planned, send a personal letter to each guest notifying him of the change or cancelation, and explain the reason for it.

Formal cancelation:

> Mr. and Mrs. James Wilson
> regret to inform you that
> due to a death in the family,
> the dinner planned for
> Friday, the twenty-fifth of August
> has been canceled.

Formal postponement:

> Mr. and Mrs. James Wilson
> sincerely regret that they must
> postpone their invitation to dinner
> On Friday, the twenty-fifth of August
> until Friday, the twenty-sixth of October
> at six-thirty o'clock
> The Boulder Inn
> Address
> due to an unexpected out-of-town business trip.

ENVELOPES

Envelopes should be of the same color and weight as the stationery or invitations. If the invitations or letters are handwritten, the envelopes should be also. Handwriting should be very neat and elegant or done in calligraphy. Neatly type the envelopes when the invitations or letters are typed. Never use computer labels on invitations. The return address goes on the front of the envelope in the upper left-hand corner, not on the back flap. For formal invitations, avoid using initials in people's names unless it is part of their name, such as in Harry S. Truman. Write out "Street," "Avenue," "Junior," "Senior" and so on, instead of using abbreviations. You should abbreviate state names, using the correct postal abbreviations.

ADDRESSING ENVELOPES

Address envelopes according to how you know the guest personally or professionally. If you know someone as a doctor, address the envelope to "Dr. So-and-So." Titles such as Mr., Mrs., and Ms. are usually used on social invitations. On business and formal invitations, they are absolutely essential and usually accompanied by professional titles. The best way to address a letter to a woman is to put her first and last name only on the outside envelope, and then put "Ms." first and her last name on the letter itself. Unless you're absolutely sure that she prefers to be addressed as "Miss" or "Mrs.," avoid using these titles; they are considered unbusinesslike. "Ms." is also the most appropriate title to use because it saves you the embarrassment of finding that you sent something addressed to a "Mrs." who isn't married, or to a "Miss" who is married.

If you're corresponding with someone you're already acquainted with, either by phone or mail, it's okay to put their first and last name or initials on the outside envelope and "Mr." or "Ms." first and last name on the inside envelope. When writing to someone whose gender you're unsure of, you may greet them with "Dear Sir or Madam."

When addressing an envelope to a husband and wife:
Mr. and Mrs. Robert Johnson
Home address

When she has kept her family name:

Mr. Robert Johnson
and Ms. Karen Scott
Home address

When he doesn't have a title, but she does:

Mr. Robert Johnson
and Dr. Karen Scott
Home address

When they have the same title:

The Doctors Johnson
Home address
or
Dr. Robert Johnson
and Dr. Karen Scott
Home address

For business or formal envelopes when no position title is used:

Ms. Karen Scott
Interior Designs by Karen
Business address

When a position title is used:

Ms. Karen Scott
President, Interior Designs by Karen
Business address

When a name is followed by a professional title:

Karen Scott, A.S.I.D.
Business address

When a name follows a title:

President Karen Scott
Interior Designs by Karen
Business address

When addressing an envelope to a couple who are living together but are not married, put their names on separate lines. Names are listed alphabetically:

Mr. Thomas Anderson
Ms. Kristen Fredericks
Address

Ms. Susan Olson
Mr. John Williams
Address

The best way to avoid wrongly addressing someone is to call the office and ask the secretary how the person prefers to be addressed. If the person's name does not identify gender, and if your future business dealings are gender-related, it is acceptable to ask the secretary for this information.

7 Thank You Notes

Not following through with thank you's is probably one of the biggest oversights salespeople can make. A thank you note can wrap up a business deal, can make you stand out from a group of interviewees, or can ensure another invitation to your host's prestigious dinners . . . a large reward for a small effort.

Sending a thank you note is more appropriate than making a phone call. Busy executives receive many phone calls each day, and your call, even with the most gracious of intentions, may interrupt an important meeting or catch the executive at an inconvenient time. A call also usually can't be shared with others in the office to whom thanks is equally due. Your thank you note shows that you took the time to express your thanks in a special way. It may be read at leisure by the recipient and others. A written thank you note usually sticks in a person's mind and helps the person to remember you in a positive way.

FUNDAMENTALS

Regardless of the nature of the occasion for which you send a thank you note, there are some thank you note fundamentals to follow:

◄ Address everyone who needs to be thanked. It's best to do this by mentioning all their names separately. If this is impractical, you can list departments or ask the person to whom the note is addressed to pass your thanks along to others.

◄ Include the name of everyone who is doing the thanking; that is, speak for the entire group.

◄ Include something particular or memorable about the event or gift. This could be how you plan to use the gift, as is true of money, how lovely the vase looks in your living room, how delicious the food was, and so on.

◄ Comment on the generosity and warmth of your host or on how much you appreciate the sender giving you exactly the gift you needed.

◄ If you stayed at your host's home for a time and met members of her family, comment on how enjoyable it was getting to know them.

◄ Thank you's are best written on formal stationery with matching envelopes or on fold over or flat cards. Cards can be plain, embossed, or with colored borders. Don't write on the card cover.

◄ A handwritten message is preferred. However, if your handwriting is hard to read, type your message.

◄ Printed thank you cards are unacceptable unless you add a personal note; otherwise they show no real appreciation. A two-or three-line handwritten message is enough, but it must be personal. A fold over card that is blank on the inside for your handwritten message works well.

◄ The purpose of a thank you note is only to thank someone. This is not the place to mention matters concerning a business deal that you forgot to say over your business lunch, or to ask for favors or contributions. Keep your note short and to the point, and don't fill it full of "thank you very much." Include it once—maximum.

GIFTS AND COMPANY BENEFITS

Even gifts you don't particularly like need to be acknowledged. You can make your note general, but try to make your appreciation apparent. Commenting positively on the gift's uniqueness is a subtle way of accomplishing this. Even though you may not like the gift, sending a thank you note is essential.

Anytime you receive a gift, a thank you note is in order. This includes not only holiday gifts and birthday gifts from associates, your company, or suppliers, but also gifts that celebrate your being with the firm for a specific period.

A thank you note needs to be sent whenever someone has done something for you. Thank you's should also be sent when you get corporate "freebies" such as tickets to sporting events or benefits, company giveaways, holiday lunches and dinners sponsored by the company, and personal use of the company condo, or yacht. Something like the following is appropriate:

> Dear Mr. Walters,
>
> What a pleasure it was to have the privilege of spending the weekend on your yacht. It was so relaxing to be out on peaceful waters, away from the hustle and bustle of the city. John and I thoroughly enjoyed the company of your staff. They were most helpful and very professionally skilled. It was a luxurious weekend we will not forget. Thank you.
>
> Mary

SOCIAL FUNCTIONS

Being invited to dinner at the home of a colleague or boss, being taken out for a business lunch or dinner, attending an extravagant party, and spending a weekend or longer at the home of a colleague or associate are additional occasions you must follow up with a written expression of your thanks. In this thank you, you'll want to mention the occasion, the fine food or decor of your host's home, your pleasure at the progress you made on the business deal and optimism for continued success, the elaborateness of the party, your host's gracious hospitality and warmth for inviting you to stay, and so on. Also mention any activities you especially enjoyed, people you met, and other memorable aspects of the event or your stay.

A sample thank you letter for a breakfast or lunch meeting could resemble the following:

> Dear Kathy,
>
> Thank you for arranging our breakfast meeting this morning! I appreciated your being so well prepared and giving your helpful comments and suggestions for content. I'm thrilled to be working with you and Robin. Together we'll have a very successful June seminar.
>
> Thank you for asking me to be the featured speaker.
>
> Very truly yours,
>
> Elizabeth Winters
> Professional Speaker

GOOD DEEDS

It's always a good idea to show those who are on your side that you appreciate their support. When a colleague stands up for you or defends you, either in your presence or in your absence, sending a thank you for her faith in your abilities and ideas is an appropriate gesture. Express your desire and willingness to reciprocate the action in the future.

INTERVIEWS

A thank you note following a job interview can make the difference between being in line for a position and getting the position. Not only will you make a good impression on the interviewer, but your name is more likely to be remembered at decision time. A typical thank you note of this variety is:

Dear Ms. Thomas,

Thank you for taking time to fit me into your busy schedule yesterday to inform me of the sales associate position open in Midwest Marketing. After listening to your description of the company and the position for which I've applied, I'm confident I can contribute to the continued success of your company.

I appreciate your consideration and optimistically wait to hear from you.

Sincerely,

Michael Harding

A sample thank you letter following a job offer that you are rejecting might read as follows:

Dear Mr. Ryan,

I want to thank you for providing me with the opportunity to come out to Denver and learn firsthand about your firm. I have carefully considered the employment offer both in Denver and in Phoenix. I am impressed with management's professional attitude towards its staff. There would appear to be considerable potential for a wide range of interests. And your compensation package is acceptable. However, as we discussed on the telephone, I am not accepting your Denver offer at this time. I have also given consideration to the position at your Phoenix branch, but again have decided not to accept the position now.

While I am interested in a career with your firm, I feel that my immediate goals are best met here in Minnesota. Perhaps the future will permit a reevaluation. Again, thank you very much for the employment offer.

Sincerely,

Bill John, P.E.

Don't hesitate to send a thank you to those who made it possible for you to get the interview and to those who were especially helpful, such as the secretary or receptionist, or an associate who gave you a tour of the office or whose shoulder you watched over for a while. Thank you's sent following a job interview are best typed and mailed no later than the day after the interview.

You also may want to thank journalists, TV or radio show producers, or the show's interviewer for doing a feature on you and your business or having you on the show. Telling your side of the story and getting free newspaper or magazine space or TV or radio air time all are good public relations tools, and if you'd like to have access to them again, sending a thank you note just might do it. In these notes, you will want to thank them for featuring you in the magazine or on the show. Complimenting the fine job done by the writer or interviewer and expressing your thanks for having your story fairly and accurately handled by professionals are effective also. If the story included falsehoods or painted an inaccurate picture of you or your company, you'll still want to thank them for featuring you, but then politely mention that some facts or statements were incorrect and list them. To conclude on a positive note, express your respect for the journalist, producer, or interviewer, and say that, although you understand that mistakes and misinterpretations happen, you would like a retraction.

A sample handwritten thank you note for a consultant to send to someone who has offered her work could be like the following:

> Dear Diane,
>
> Thank you so much for your telephone call yesterday and for thinking of me to be involved in your project. It is a terrific idea. I certainly hope it gets funded.
>
> I am looking forward to working with you and Becky on this and other future projects. I appreciate your keeping me in mind.
>
> Very truly yours,
>
> Linda James

TIMELINESS

The standard amount of time for sending a thank you note after receiving a gift or attending an event is preferably within one week. Still, better late than never! Thank you's tend to be appreciated more when sent while the gift or event is still fresh in everyone's mind. If a gift is sent by mail it's best to send a thank you as soon as possible so the sender knows you received the gift. Do not overdo your thank you's. One is enough. Sending a thank you for a thank you or a thank you for a gift that was sent as a thank you is getting carried away.

8 Table Manners

Are you frazzled by forks? Nervous about napkins? Frightened by formalities? Relax! Learning proper table manners isn't as intimidating as you may think. It's only a matter of common sense, and with just a little practice, you can have your table manners perfected in no time.

There is no getting away from the need for good table manners, and knowing how to act at a dinner table is going to make your job of being a guest or gracious host a lot easier and more enjoyable—not to mention the favorable impression you'll make on others.

A fundamental tip for table manners is to follow the host's lead. After she takes the first bite of her food, you may begin eating.

The host is the first to begin eating, unless she tells you to eat so your food doesn't get cold.

UNMANNERLY MANNERS

One downfall of many executives is table manners. Your lunch or dinner host or guest is likely to notice that you put too much food into your mouth, that you talked with your mouth full, or that you didn't use the silverware for the food it was intended to be used for. Don't pile too much food on your plate, because doing so is likely to make you eat faster, which will lead to your talking with your mouth full.

Also, drinking too much alcohol when dining out is one of the most-disliked business behaviors.

Although you've probably heard it since childhood, sitting up straight at the table still makes a good impression. Sit up straight, but not stiffly. Men, make sure all the women are seated before you sit. When you're not eating, hands may be kept in your lap—not playing with silverware, not putting on makeup, not straightening your hair or otherwise fidgeting. Elbows may rest gently on the edge of the table between courses, but not while you're eating. Don't take up more elbow room than you need while eating; be considerate of your neighbors.

One of the most basic but perhaps the most important thing to remember when at the table is to never chew with your mouth open or make loud noises when you eat. Listening to someone smacking their lips is generally not appreciated.

Cutting your salad is definitely acceptable, not to mention preferable to getting salad dressing all over your face or trying to shove a big lettuce leaf into your mouth. When cutting meat, salad, or any other food, cut enough for two or three mouthfuls and eat those before cutting more. Don't cut up your whole steak at once. That is done only for children.

In the United States, slurping soup from a spoon just won't do. Spoon the soup away from you when you take it out of the bowl, lean slightly forward to meet the spoonful, and sip the soup from the side of the spoon. If your soup is too hot to eat, stir it gently with your spoon; don't blow on it.

Don't slurp your coffee, and make sure you swallow before you speak. Place a used teabag beside your cup on your saucer. Remember, it's all a matter of common sense made common practice.

If your fork or spoon finds its way to the floor, pick it up if you can reach it and let the server know you need a clean one. If you are unable to reach it, tell the server you dropped yours and request a clean one.

If the silverware is dirty, get your server's attention and ask her for a clean one.

If you receive terrible service or food, ask to speak with the manager and discuss the issue with him. Do not make a scene or yell at the server.

Other unmannerly behaviors include wadding up your dirty napkin and leaving it on your plate—or crumpling up your napkin at all. Fold it loosely and leave it beside your plate. Leaving the spoon in your coffee cup or soup bowl ranks high on the list of taboos, too. Businesswomen who wear lipstick should use it in moderation when dining out and blot their lips before drinking from a cup or glass. It's inappropriate to leave a lipstick mark.

If you're hosting a lunch or dinner, it's most impolite to arrive later than your guests and to leave them guessing what price range they may order from. If you're a guest at a lunch or dinner, don't take it upon yourself to invite others or to order the most expensive item on the menu.

SPECIAL EATING REQUIREMENTS

If you are invited to a dinner and have special eating requirements, let your host know of them when you accept the invitation. This gives her time to adjust the menu. It's also acceptable, and probably much easier for both of you, if you offer to bring your container of food that can be quickly heated up. This will allow you to attend the party, yet it will save the host from having to change the menu or prepare something special for you.

ARRIVING EARLY

What to do before your guests or host arrive for a business dinner or lunch is a problem many people face. You have several options here, both as a host and as a guest. When deciding what to do while you're waiting, consider whom you're meeting and the nature of the dinner or lunch.

If you're the host, you must arrive before your guests to ensure that your table is ready and that everything is in order. You may wait by the door for your guest to arrive so you can walk with him to your table. If you can see the entryway from your table, it's acceptable to sit at your table while waiting for your guest to arrive, and then rise to greet him or make a small motion with your hand to get his attention. It would be very helpful to let your guest know the location of "your table" (if you have one) in the dining room beforehand, so he will know approximately where to find you. Another option is to wait at your table and have the maitre d' show your guest to it if you can't see the entryway.

Whether you're the host or the guest, if you're waiting at a table, it's best not to order anything to eat or drink. The table must look as though it hasn't been used. It is acceptable to drink some of your water, however. If the other party has not arrived in fifteen to twenty minutes from the indicated time, something has probably come up to delay them. Call the office of the overdue person after fifteen minutes. After a reasonable wait, you can either order your meal or leave. If you choose to leave, be sure to leave a message so that if the person arrives, she will not wait for you.

Being late for business lunches or dinners isn't a good habit to get into, especially if you're the host. There is no such thing as "fashionably late" in the business world, and neither party needs to wait longer than fifteen minutes for the other to arrive. If you're late because of circumstances beyond your control or for a very valid reason, apologize and explain the situation to your associate. If it should happen that the other party—host or guest—never shows, the server still needs to be tipped for the use of the table. If something unexpected arises and you need to cancel your appointment for a business lunch it is fine to reschedule. A deadline, an important meeting or another business crisis, inclement weather, and feeling ill are all possible reasons why you may need to cancel a scheduled meal. It is okay to cancel the morning of the appointment.

If you do cancel, it is your responsibility to reschedule. If you want to cancel because of bad weather, be sure to let the other person know the reason and ask if rescheduling is acceptable to her. If it is not, you must keep the appointment. If you're unable to cancel the appointment and have someone else do it for you, get back to the person, apologize, explain, and attempt to reschedule.

INAPPROPRIATE GUEST BEHAVIOR

If your guest becomes drunk or obnoxious, speaks too loudly, or is otherwise rude, end the lunch as quickly as possible. Make up an excuse such as, "I have a meeting at the office I have to get back to," pay the tab, and leave. You are not responsible for your guest's behavior, nor do you have to be embarrassed by him. If you suspect the problem is alcohol related you may choose to notify the maitre d' on your way out. Then forget that the incident ever happened.

NAPKIN SENSE

The meal begins when the host starts to unfold her napkin. This is the signal for you to do the same. Typically you want to put your napkin on your lap within the first ten seconds after sitting down at the table, and don't remove it until you are ready to leave the table. However, follow the host's lead. The napkin should be unfolded if it's small and partially unfolded if it's large, then laid across your lap. A napkin is not to be used as a bib unless you're under two years of age, wearing a paper bib supplied by lobster restaurants, or eating a meal that includes much sauce. If you're the host, let your guests know what is acceptable napkin behavior through example.

A second "never" in table manners is to never use your napkin as a handkerchief unless it's an absolute emergency, especially if the napkins are made of cloth. Women need to be careful not to get lipstick on cloth napkins, as it can stain. Your napkin remains on your lap throughout the meal and is used to blot, not wipe, your mouth. If you must leave the table during the meal, place your napkin on your chair. The host will signal the end of the meal by placing her napkin on the table.

"I'M FINISHED" SIGNAL

Do not push your plate away from you when you are done with your meal. Just leave it where it is in the place setting. The standard way to show that you've finished with your meal is to lay your fork and knife diagonally across your plate. Put your dinner fork and knife side by side diagonally across your plate, as if they are pointing to 10, with the handles on the 4. The handles point toward the 4, and the blade of the knife faces inward. If you are merely letting your food settle or need to leave the table, cross your fork and knife on your plate, making an X.

DOGGY BAGS

Whether you want to ask for a doggy bag depends on the situation. Will you be going on to other meetings after the meal or back to a hotel room that does not have a refrigerator? Additionally, consider your host's preference. Some executives do not feel it is professional to ask for a container in which to take food. Others feel that not wasting food is the right thing to do.

THE TAB

When there is no established host or when you are traveling, the most senior professional in the group usually picks up the tab. On the other hand, if you hold a less senior position and you would like to pay for something, it is acceptable to pay the bar tab, leave the tip, or pay other small tabs.

If a business associate is uneasy about letting the other person pay for the meal, prevent any feelings of tension by asking the maitre d' before the guest's arrival to give you the check. Or, you can tell your associates, my company is picking up the tab, not I.

You may be able to eliminate the need for the check to be brought to the table at all. When you call in to make your reservation you can provide your credit card information at that time, or on your arrival, check with the maitre d' to see if you can charge the meal to your credit card and instruct them to add their standard service charge or a 15 percent tip. Since you have already signed, paying for the meal is taken care of, and there is no discussion or uneasiness about who should pay.

If you can't arrive early but can get away from the table graciously during the meal, you can take that opportunity to pay the bill before it is brought to your table. Remember, it is always unprofessional to fight over the tab.

9 Solutions to "Sticky" Situations

We've all been in those situations where the person you were having lunch with had a bit of food stuck on his face or in his teeth. Or you dropped a piece of silverware under the table and were unable to reach it. Or you took a bite of food that was still too hot and had to take it out of your mouth. Whatever the awkward situation, knowing how to handle it gracefully can make the difference between whether people forget it or never let you live it down.

FOOD AND BEVERAGE SPILLS

"Don't cry over spilt milk" is a common saying that holds true for table manners. If you do spill something on your lap, tie, or shirt, simply use a clean knife or wet a small corner of your napkin in your water glass to remove or absorb the spill. Crying, shouting, or getting upset will only call attention to you and make the situation worse. If you happen to spill on the tablecloth, don't cover it with your plate. Wipe up the spill with your napkin, and tell the host or server so he can take whatever action is necessary to prevent the spill from staining.

REMOVING UNWANTED FOOD

You knew the second you took the fork out of your mouth that the food was still too hot to eat. Your tongue and mouth are burning. What do you do? Taking a drink of water or another cold beverage is the best way to remain cool, calm, and collected. If you discover a bone, fruit pit, or piece of gristle while chewing, remove it the same way it went in. For example, if you're eating with your fork, remove the object by placing it on your fork and then onto the side of your plate. Objects such as fish bones are easier to remove with your thumb and forefinger. Use whichever method will draw the least attention to yourself. Don't remove the object by spitting it into your napkin, especially if it's a cloth napkin. If you take a bite of something you don't like, swallow it as quickly as possible, but if something is spoiled, by all means remove it. Use whatever utensil you put the food in with, and remove it the same way it went in. To remove food that is stuck in your teeth, excuse yourself, go to the rest room, and remove it there.

SOILED SILVERWARE

Getting a piece of soiled silverware is no cause for alarm. If you're in a restaurant, simply ask the server for a clean utensil. If you're at a dinner party, ask the host for a clean one. Dropping a piece of silverware is also not a big deal. Pick it up if you can reach it, and ask the server for a clean one. If it's out of your reach, let the server know you dropped it, and she will pick it up after everyone has left. Picking up a dropped utensil, wiping it off with your napkin, and placing it on the table where no one will use it is acceptable at a dinner party.

SNEEZING AT THE TABLE

Right in the middle of the second course, it happens. Your nose starts to tingle and itch, your eyes water—you're going to sneeze. You can't stop it, but you can prevent it from offending others. Turn your head away from the table and away from all others if possible, and put your handkerchief or hand over your mouth and nose when you sneeze. If you must blow your nose, excuse yourself from the table. If you cannot be excused, turn your head away and do it quickly and quietly.

TOOTHPICKS

It's difficult to say which is more embarrassing—being the one with the food stuck in her teeth or being the one to tell someone else that they have food stuck somewhere it shouldn't be. Do you pretend you don't notice it and hope that the person will go to the rest room soon and notice it for herself? Or do you rub your chin or face and hope the person gets the message? Neither of these methods is going to make you comfortable, since the food particle is still there. The best way to handle this is to simply tell the person quietly. If you're on the receiving end of such a message, thank the person for telling you, excuse yourself, and go to the rest room to remove the food from your teeth, or use your napkin to remove it from your face. While at the table, don't use toothpicks or try to remove the food from your teeth with your tongue or fingers. If you're dining with family members or in a very casual setting, the discreet use of toothpicks may be permissible, but it isn't recommended.

ORTHODONTIC APPLIANCES

Many adults now have braces. When you're wearing braces, proper etiquette and common sense demand that you keep them clean. Watch what you eat so you don't have food caught in or hanging from them. If you're a woman, you will also want to keep lipstick off your braces. A tinted gloss doesn't show up as much when it does get on the appliances.

Besides toothbrush and toothpaste, there are other items made for keeping your braces clean. A small, round-head brush made especially to fit under your archwire fits into little spaces that a regular toothbrush can't and works well for removing food from under your wires and from your brackets. It's also a good idea to keep a supply of dental floss on hand. If your teeth are so close together that floss won't fit between them, or if your braces make it difficult for you to get the floss between your teeth, ask your orthodontist about using a floss threader.

Toothpicks are especially helpful for removing food that is tightly lodged in your brackets, and is also terrific for a quick cleaning if you are not able to brush. Though your whole mouth won't be clean, at least you can get the lettuce out of your braces. No matter which tool you use to keep your braces clean, always check in a mirror to make sure you did get all the food particles out.

Your orthodontist told you to avoid these foods because they can damage your braces, but you might want to avoid them just because of the potentially embarrassing situations they also can put you in. Grape juice, tea, and coffee stain porcelain and plastic braces. If you eat hard foods such as nuts, popcorn, and corn chips or tortilla chips, you're just asking for them to get stuck in your brackets. Gum, taffy, caramels and other gooey foods are trouble too. Peel raw fruits such as apples and cut them up into small pieces. They're easier to eat that way, and you won't have to worry about having pieces of red apple peel stuck between your teeth. Raw vegetables are also easiest to eat when cut into small pieces. Forget corn on the cob. Bread and rolls, especially those with a hard crust, can be troublemakers too. Instead of biting into that sandwich with your teeth, break off bite-sized pieces with your fingers and place them into your mouth. Or, cut your sandwich into bite-sized pieces and then eat them using your fork. This is probably the most acceptable, especially when out on a business luncheon.

Vegetables such as lettuce, broccoli (those darned little green buds!), and cauliflower can be tricky. They're all great ones for getting stuck in brackets and behind wires. Your best bet is to cut lettuce into little pieces; a food processor can come in handy for this. With broccoli and cauliflower, everyone is on their own. If you discover a way to eat these vegetables without getting them stuck in your braces, there are many people wearing braces who would like to know how you do it.

SMOKING

Smoking is becoming a touchy subject these days, particularly with secondhand smoke being identified as the cause of certain illnesses in nonsmokers. If you are a smoker, it is best to smoke only in your own home. When in public, even in a business office, always ask if you may smoke. If you're the host or conducting the business meeting, let individuals know what your policy is regarding smoking.

Many people find smoking offensive even if they don't say so, so even if given the go-ahead, be considerate of others. You might consider excusing yourself from the table and stepping outside to smoke. If you do stay at the table to smoke, let everyone finish their meal before you smoke, and again be sure it is okay with everyone. If your host has ashtrays on the table, it's probably okay for you to smoke before dessert and after the meal, but not between courses. Even if the host has given the go-ahead, there may be some guests who do not want you to smoke. Again, be sure to ask, and be considerate.

10 Menu Ordering

"May I take your order?" When the server asks this question, do you and your guests all look at each other wondering who will give their order first? Are there several "You go first. No, you go first" heard? If there are, it's time to put some order into your ordering.

This chapter will help you with the variety of questions that come up regarding the menu and service you would like to receive.

QUESTIONS ABOUT THE MENU

If, after looking over the menu, there are any items you are uncertain of—whether you're wondering about what they are, how they're prepared, how to pronounce their names, or whatever—feel free to ask your server any questions you may have. Answering them is part of their job. It's better to find out before you order than to order what turns out to be chicken livers, when you hate chicken livers, or to find out that your fish will be served with its head still on and its eyes staring at you throughout your meal.

Ask about the service and anything on the menu you're unsure of. Remember, the only stupid question is the one that goes unasked. Keep in mind also that as the customer, you're the boss. The restaurant is there to serve you, and without you, it wouldn't be in business. Feel free to ask questions whether you're at an expensive French restaurant or your local fast-food joint. Of course, you're not as likely to be intimidated by or ask as many questions at a fast-food restaurant as you would an expensive foreign restaurant. Fast-food menus are usually simple and straightforward.

Cheeseburgers, french fries, and soft drinks are easy for most people to pronounce, and you know what you're getting. French, Italian, Chinese and other foreign restaurants may be another story. Unless you are fluent in these languages or have eaten at these types of restaurants before, you'll probably need to ask questions about items on the menu or about the service.

Eating at an expensive restaurant can be a little nerve rattling for anyone who's never done it before. And looking at the menu and realizing you can't pronounce or understand a word on it may tempt you to make a mad dash for the nearest door. If you know you will be dining at an exclusive restaurant, you can prepare ahead of time by consulting Chapter 11, "Menu Terms."

Restaurant employees are also there to help you, and you are wise to take advantage of their knowledge. Often you will come across words you can't pronounce and you don't have a clue as to what they are, or you'll have a vague idea about what a dish is, but you don't know how it's served. These are exactly the times to ask a captain or server.

If, after you have tasted your meal, you find it unacceptable, let your server know. You have a right to expect and receive a good meal for the price you're paying.

To get your server's attention, saying "Excuse me" when he is nearby, waving your hand slightly when he is looking toward you, or asking a nearby employee to notify him that you request his assistance are the most polite methods. To show that you're ready to order, close your menu and place it on the table.

ORDERING SEQUENCE

How you order will depend upon whether you're the host or a guest, what type of meal you're going to be eating, how many people are at the table, and whether your guests are male or female. The host is the person who will be paying the check. His order is generally taken last. If a man asks a woman out, he is the host and vice versa. The guest's order is placed first.

When people are dining out together as a group, the server may decide how the ordering will proceed by selecting the method that is the most efficient. Normally, the women's orders are taken first, with each woman individually giving her order to the server. The men's orders follow. The host's order is taken last. Again, be sure to let the server know if there will be one check or separate ones. People paying individually for their meals, when they are on one check, should keep track of how much the entire meal is going to cost before the menus are removed. If everyone is ordering approximately the same items with the same costs, the bill should be divided equally.

APPETIZERS—THE FIRST COURSE

The first course may consist of an appetizer, or hors d'oeuvres. This course is usually kept light and simple, not only because people don't want to be full before the second course arrives, but also because more people have become conscious of their weight and health. Some possible appetizers or hors d'oeuvres are quiche, pâté, fresh vegetables served with dip, fresh fruit, and cheese and crackers or cheese sticks. If your entrée is going to be very filling, you may want to omit the first course.

SOUP—THE SECOND COURSE

Soup can be served as the first course, but soup often is a course in itself. Soups can be heavy or light, served hot or cold. When ordering a heavy soup such as a cream soup, keep your entrée light. A meat with vegetables would be enough. Having potatoes or rice would be too much. A light soup has a broth base and is a good choice on those occasions when you want to have a heavier entrée, perhaps with potatoes or rice. Hot soups are especially welcome on cold days, and chilled soups are refreshing on hot days. Some soups are served either hot or cold, regardless of the temperature outside.

And remember, do not break crackers into your soup. When crackers are served, break off a bite-sized portion and place the remaining cracker on the underplate.

SALAD—THE THIRD COURSE

Or is it the fourth? Depending on when the restaurant serves it, the salad may come either before or after the entrée. At more formal banquets and restaurants, salad is served at the more traditional time: after the entrée.

The salad fork and knife are those closest to the plate, but if the entrée and the salad are served at the same time, go ahead and use the entrée fork for both. After the salad, your plate is removed, and this is the only time, in a more formal setting, that you will be without a plate in front of you during the whole meal.

THE ENTRÉE—THE FOURTH COURSE

Or is it the third? Whether the entrée is served as the third or fourth course, you may want to decide which way of eating you'll use: the American or European style. Both are discussed in more detail in Chapter 13, "Coping with Tableware."

Just a word about salt and pepper: If someone asks for the salt, pass both the salt and pepper together. Also, experienced diners taste their food first before adding salt.

DESSERT—THE FIFTH COURSE

When someone says the word *dessert,* images of rich, gooey, chocolate morsels, filled with whipped or ice cream. immediately come to mind. But this doesn't have to be the case. Depending upon what you ordered for the rest of the courses, your dessert may need to be very light. A heavy entrée needs to be topped off with a light dessert, or heaven forbid for some, no dessert at all. Fruit and cheeses are a possibility. Yet, if the meal was light, go ahead and order that cream puff drowned in chocolate sauce and ice cream.

Some weight watchers will forget their diets when it comes to having dessert; others won't. Some people would prefer not to cry when they step on the scale the next morning. Dessert is typically included in more formal meals, though.

THE HOST'S ROLE

When a woman asks a man out, she is the host. She asks the server for the menus. She may place her order first and then ask her guest what he would like. He then gives his order to the server. At a business luncheon, the woman always places her own order, even if she is a guest.

When two men or two women are dining out as friends and having the same item, either person may order for both of them. If ordering different items, the guest orders first. If neither person is the guest, the older individual places her order first. Be sure to establish with the server who the check should go to or if separate checks are needed.

WHICH ITEM TO ORDER

As a guest, don't order one of the most expensive items or more than two courses unless your host suggests that it's all right. If he says something like, "I'm going to have the lobster; I think you'd enjoy it also," or "I'm going to have this new dessert; why don't you try it too," then it's okay to order that item if you'd like. Also, it's not a good idea to order a first course if no one else has. They might be on a tight time schedule and don't have time to linger over a long, drawn-out lunch.

If you're the host, make these decisions easier for your guests by letting them know what and how many courses you plan to order. It's also your duty as a host to make sure that a main course has been decided upon before a wine is selected.

TIMING THE MEAL

If you are dining before attending another engagement and are on a schedule or having a five-course meal with someone special, it's perfectly acceptable to speed up or slow down the pace of the meal. Simply let your server know that you are on a tight time schedule and would like to order something that can be prepared in a short amount of time. There is no need to be rude and say, "Step on it. We're in a hurry!" A simple, "We have an engagement we have to be at by 7:00 P.M., so we need to be done with our meal by 6:15 P.M.," is fine.

She will be able to suggest items that can be prepared within your time limit. If, on the other hand, you want to lengthen your mealtime, let your server know that you'd like to finish your drinks before you order your first course and that there is no need to rush between courses.

Checking Your Check

Don't hesitate to examine your check for errors. When you are ordering your meal, look at the menu and try to remember the price. Unfortunately, restaurants do make mistakes on checks. If your bill seems larger than you expected, ask your server about the charges.

Beware À La Carte

Unknown to you, your meal may have been "à la carte." If it was, then you were charged for each course or additional item separately instead of being charged one price for the entire meal. À la carte meals are usually more expensive. The best way to avoid this shock is to read your menu carefully. Although they're supposed to be, prices aren't always clearly listed. The menu may not show that items are a la carte or clearly show extra charges. Be sure to read all the small print. This is usually where restaurants will indicate extra charges and other information that you may want to know. If you're still confused after thoroughly reading the menu, ask!

Any time you encounter a menu misrepresentation, it is acceptable and your right to do something about it. If you feel your meal is inferior in any way, whether the portion is smaller than described, the fruit is canned instead of fresh, or whatever, don't hesitate to discuss the issue with the manager.

11 Menu
Terms

Agneau (ah NYOH) — French for "lamb."

Ail (AH yuh) — French for "garlic."

À la Anglaise (ah lah AN glez) — French, "prepared in water or stock."

À la Carte (ah lah KART) — in the style of the menu. Each part of a meal or dish, such as soup, salad, extra cheese on a sandwich, and so on is individually priced. À la carte meals usually cost more than meals that are listed under one price.

À la Maison (ah lah ma ZAHn) — "according to the house." Describes how items will be prepared at a particular restaurant. Restaurants all have different styles, so the same item may be prepared differently at different restaurants.

Amandine (ah mahn DEEN) — "with almonds," often used in Chinese and fish dishes

Antipasto (an ti PAS to) — Italian for "appetizer."

Au gratin (oh GRAH tin) — served with bread crumbs and/or cheese on top.

Au jus (oh ZHOO) — in its own natural juices.

Au poivre (oh PWAHV ruh) — French, "with pepper."

Béarnaise (behr NEHZ) — French, a heavy sauce consisting of egg yolks, butter, wine vinegar, terragon, thyme, and shallots served over eggs or meat.

Beurre (BUHR) — French for "butter."

Bisque (BISK) — French, a thick cream soup consisting of shellfish and spices.

Boeuf (BUHF) — French for "beef."

Blue Points — oysters from Blue Point, Long Island, New York.

Bordelaise (bohr DLEHZ) — French, a red wine sauce consisting of shallots, butter, tomatoes, onions, and beef marrow.

Bouillabaisse (boo yuh BEHZ) — a Mediterranean fish stew.

Bouillon (boo YON) — clear broth.

Boursin (boor SAn) — French, a creamy cheese often flavored with garlic, herbs, fruit, or seeds.

Brie (BREE) — semisoft cheese.

Brioche (bree OSH) — French yeast roll that can be served for breakfast, is hollowed out and filled with creamed meat or poultry.

Brochette (broh SHET) — French for "skewer."

Caesar Salad — a salad made of Romaine lettuce, Parmesan cheese, olive oil, egg, lemon, and spices that is usually tossed at your table.

Camembert (kah mehn BEHR) — a pungently flavored semi-soft cheese.

Canapés (CAN na PEE) — French, an appetizer consisting of small pieces of bread topped with various spreads.

Cappuccino (cap pa CHEE no) — an Italian coffee made of hot milk and strong black coffee.

Champignons (shan peen YOHn) — French for "mushrooms."

Chateâubriand (shah toh bree AHn) — French, a thick cut of grilled sirloin or Porterhouse steak served with vegetables and sauce.

Chez (SHAY) — see "À la Maison."

Chocolat (shah koh LAH) — French for "chocolate."

Consommé (kahn soh MAY) — clear, seasoned broth.

Coq au vin (koh koh VAn) — French, chicken, mushrooms, garlic, onions, and diced pork in a red wine sauce.

Coquilles St. Jacques (koh KEE yuh san ZHAHK) — French, scallops in white wine sauce topped with cheese and served in a scallop shell.

Cordon Bleu (kohr dahn BLUE) — Swiss for "blue ribbon." Items stuffed or served with Swiss cheese.

Crème (KREHM) — French for "cream."

Crêpe (KREHP) — French, thin pancakes.

Croissant (kwah SAHn) — crescent-shaped French roll.

Crudités (kroo dee TAY) — French, an appetizer of raw vegetables and dip.

Dessert (da SEHR) — French for "dessert."

Du jour (du ZHOOR) — French for "of the day," such as "soup du jour."

En croûte (ahn KROOT) — French for "in a crust."

Entrée (an TRA) — French for "main course."

Escargots (es kahr GOH) — French for "snails."

Fettuccine (fet a CHEE NEE) — Italian ribbon noodles.

Filet mignon (fil LAY meen YAWN) — French for a small, thick steak from the beef tenderloin.

Flambe (flam BAY) — French for "flamed."

Florentine (floh rehn TEEN) — a French cooking style in which food is served on spinach and topped with a cream sauce and grated cheese.

Fondue (fon DUE) — Swiss style of dipping food into a hot pot of oil or cheese with special forks.

Fromage (froh MAHZH) — French for "cheese."

Gâteau (gah TO) — French for "cake."

Half-shell — raw shellfish served with a sauce.

Herbe (EHRB) — French for "herb."

Hollandaise (HAHL uhn daz) — a rich sauce of egg yolks, butter, lemon, and vinegar.

Hors d'oeuvres (ohr DURV) — appetizers.

Julienne (zhoo LYEHN) — meat or vegetables cut into sticks or shreds.

Lait (LAY) — French for "milk."

Laitue (la TOO) — French for "lettuce."

Légumes (lay GYUME) — French for "vegetables."

Mornay (mohr NAY) — French, a sauce made of butter, flour, broth, cream, and cheese.

Mousse (MOOS) — a French dish with a smooth, whipped texture, as in "chocolate mousse."

Niçoise (nee SWAHZ) — French, with tomatoes and garlic and possibly black olives, onions, and peppers.

Nouilles (noo EE) — French for "noodles."

Oeufs (UH) — French for "eggs."

Oignon (oin YOHN) — French for "onion."

Omelette (ahm LEHT) — a French plain or filled egg dish; omelet.

Pain (pan) — French for "bread."

Pasta — Italian noodlelike product; includes macaroni, spaghetti, fettuccine, and tortellini.

Pâté (pah TAY) — French, a paste of finely ground meat and seasonings.

Pâtisserie (pah tee SREE) — French for "pastry."

Petits-fours (peh tee FOOR) — French, "little cakes."

Poisson (pwah SOHn) — French for "fish."

Pomme (PUHM) — French for "apple."

Pomme de terre (puhm duh TEHR) — French, "potato."

Potage (poh TAHZH) — French soup.

Poulet (poo LAY) — French, "chicken."

Prawn — large shrimp.

Prix fixe (pree FEEX) — French for "fixed price," a set price.

Prosciutto (proh SHOO TO) — Italian, salted but not smoked ham.

Provencale (proh VEHn SAHL) — French, cooked with tomatoes, garlic, and olive oil.

Purée (pyoor RAY) — whipped to a pastelike consistency.

Quenelles (kuh NEHL) — French, dumplings of poached fish or meat.

Quiche Lorraine (keesh loh REHN) — French, a tart consisting of cream, eggs, cheese, and bacon.

Rarebit (RARE bit) — British, a cheese dish served over toast.

Ratatouille (rah tah TOO ee) — a French dish of eggplant, zucchini, squash, onion, tomato, and pepper.

Ris de veau (ree duh VOH) — French, pancreas of calf or lamb sweetbreads.

Rix (REE) — French for "rice."

Roquefort (rohk FOHR) — blue cheese.

Roti (roh TEE) — French for "roasted."

Salade (sah LAHD) — French for "salad."

Salisbury steak — a patty of ground beef.

Sauerbraten — German, roast beef marinated in vinegar and served with a sweet and sour sauce.

Saumon (soh MAHn) — French for "salmon."

Sauté (soh TAY) — to cook quickly in fat.

Sel — French for "salt."

Sorbet (sohr BAY) — French for "sherbet." A tart ice.

Soufflé (soo FLAY) — French for "puffed up." A baked dish of whipped eggs and flavorings.

Steak Diane — thin steak sautéed or flamed in butter and sherry sauce at your table.

Steak Tartare (tahr TAHR) — raw ground beef that has been ground twice, had seasonings added, and is topped with a raw egg yolk.

Table d'hote (tabl doht) — French for "host's table," an entire meal (all courses) is served for one price.

Terrine (tehr REEN) — French, a pâté-like dish.

Thé (TAY) — French for "tea."

Tomates (toh MAHT) — French for "tomatoes."

Veau (VOH) — French for "veal."

Viande (VYAHND) — French for "meat."

Vichyssoise (vee shee SWAHZ) — a cold cream, chicken stock, leek, and potato soup.

Vinaigrette (vee neh GREHT) — an oil and vinegar dressing.

Vin (VAn) — French for "wine."

Vin, blanc (van BLAHn) — French for "white wine."

Vin rouge (van ROOZH) — French for "red wine."

Welsh rarebit (Welsh RARE bit) — see "rarebit."

Wienerschnitzel (VEE ner shnit sel) — sliced veal dipped in batter and sautéed.

12 Wine Basics

Not only are the names of wines often difficult to pronounce, but selecting them can be even more challenging. Entertaining an important client or guests can turn out to be a not-so-impressive experience if you're not familiar with ordering and knowing what to do with wines once they arrive at the table. Fortunately, there are people you can turn to for help.

SELECTION

The sommelier, or wine steward, is the person who takes your wine order. She presents you with the list from which you make your selection. Order wine after you have chosen your meal. If you're unsure of the best wine to complement your meal, feel free to ask the wine steward for a recommendation. Let her know what your meal will consist of and approximately what price range you'd like to stay in. If there is a member of your party who is especially knowledgeable about wines, it is perfectly acceptable to hand the wine list to her and let her make the selection. Another good idea is to ask your guests if they prefer a particular wine.

White wine formerly was served only with white meat, such as fish and chicken, and red wine was served only with red meats such as beef, pork, and game. That is not necessarily a steadfast rule anymore. In general, red wine is heavier and is served with heavier meals, while white wine is a lighter wine to be served with lighter meals. Still, some people prefer only red or white wine regardless of the meal being served. If you consider your meal, your guest's preferences, the wine steward's recommendations, and your knowledge about wine, your selection will be fine.

When choosing wine, either contrast or complement the food. One of the most important points I have ever learned about selecting wine is that it is difficult to serve great food and great wine simultaneously. You need to do one or the other.

RITUALS

Red wine is best served at room temperature, with at least half an hour of "breathing" time before being served with the meal. This time allows the wine to breathe and fully develop its flavor. White wine, because it is lighter, can be served before the meal arrives and is best served chilled. It doesn't have to "breathe" because it doesn't develop a bouquet like red wine does.

Before a bottle of red wine is brought to the table, it is uncorked. The steward then brings the bottle of wine and the cork to the table and presents both to the host or whomever did the ordering. The person receiving the wine checks the label to make sure it's the one she ordered, pinches the cork to check for moisture to make sure it is not dried out, and smells the cork to make sure it does not smell like vinegar. After nodding her approval to the steward, the steward pours a small amount of wine into the person's wine glass. At this point, the person sniffs the wine to check the bouquet, takes a sip, and indicates again to the steward that it's acceptable. The person who ordered the wine is the first to taste it, for two reasons. First, it ensures that the wine is acceptable. Second, this way the host, not one of the guests, receives any small pieces of cork that may be left in the neck of the bottle. The steward then fills everyone's wine glass half full, serving the host last.

The host follows the same procedure when ordering white wine, except that it is not necessary to smell the wine's bouquet because white wine doesn't develop a bouquet as fully as red wine does.

Following the wine rituals when you're not sure of what you are doing may make you feel ridiculous. If you're not sure you can pull this off smoothly, look at the cork to see that it is not dried out, and smell it to make sure it does not smell vinegary. Say to the steward, "I'm sure it is fine. Please just go ahead and pour it for everyone."

If the server brings you the correct bottle, yet the wine turns out to be different than you expected, just drink it. Send (or attempt to send) a bottle of wine back only if it is genuinely bad. If it smells skunky, tastes vinegary, moldy, rubbery, or is chemical tasting, these are some of the sure signs of bad wine.

WINE TASTING

If you're not as knowledgeable about wines as you'd like to be, there are several ways you can become more familiar with them. Wine tasting is a reliable way to learn about wines. Tasting enables you to decide which wines you prefer. It also provides you with the opportunity to sample the wines with a variety of foods to discover your favorite combinations. You might even want to get together with friends just to compare preferences. Your wine dealer is another good source of information. She can provide information on vintages, prices, and which wines best complement certain foods. Reading books and magazines on wine is also helpful for learning about types, vintages, prices, and which wines to serve with which foods.

Should you be invited to a business function where wine tasting is going on, be assured that spitting is the norm. Wine tasting is the one place in our culture where it is polite to spit. In fact, it is foolish not to. You can guess that if you drink all of every wine presented (often there can be eight to ten different wines), you will become intoxicated fairly quickly.

WINES AND CHEESES

If you're going out for a light lunch or looking for a fun finger food for guests, try wine and cheese. Wine goes very well not only with five-course meals, but also with a simple snack like cheese and crackers. Red wines, because they are heavier than white wines, are generally served with stronger cheeses. White wines accompany milder cheeses. Roquefort (ROHK-fuhrt) and other blue-veined cheeses are best complemented by a full-flavored Burgundy or port. Beaujolais (boh-zhoh-LAY) or Médoc (may-dawk), two red wines, go well with crusted soft cheeses. If you prefer mild cream cheese, try a Moselle (mo-ZELL<RM>, MO-z'l) or another medium dry wine. A stronger white wine—white Burgundy or dry champagne, for example—is appropriate for stronger soft cheeses. Red wine, sherry, and port all go well with Cheddar cheese. Mild Fontina (fahn-TEE-nah) cheese or Bel Paese (BELL pah-AY-zay) cheese is good to serve with an Italian Soave (swa-vay), and Gorgonzola (gohr-guhn-ZOH-lah) cheese and Chianti (kee-AHN-tee) are a very palatable combination.

It's best to eat the cheese on plain, unflavored bread or crackers so it doesn't interfere with the flavor of the cheese and wine. To add a little variety to your wine and cheese lunch or snack, include fruits and vegetables such as apples, pears, grapes, celery, cucumber, and carrot sticks.

Cabernet Sauvignon (SO-veen-YAWN)

Cabernet Sauvignon grapes produce elegant red wines with flavors often similar to tea, olives, leaves, currants, or herbs.

Chardonnay (shar-duh-NAY)

Chardonnay grapes are the most famous in the world for producing dry white wine. Some great white wines produced with the chardonnay grape are all the great white Burgundies—Meursault (mere-SO, Montrachet (mohn-truh-SHAY), Pouilly-Fuissé (poo-YE fwee-SAY) and Chablis (sha-BLEE; pl. sha-BLEEZ). It is one of the grapes used in Brut Champagne (brute sham-PAYN) and the only grape used to make Blanc de Blancs (BLAHNGK deh BLAHNGK) champagne. Chardonnay wines are a great choice with poached white fish, because it is light bodied and doesn't fight with the taste of the fish.

Chenin Blanc (SHEN-ihn BLAHNGK)

Chenin Blanc grapes make white wines that range from bone dry to very sweet. Through all its versions it retains a well-defined fruitiness, often suggestive of pear. It has a pleasant crispness because of its high degree of acidity.

Gewürztraminer (geh-VOORTS-truh-mee-nuhr)

This white grape yields a pungent, spicy white wine with hints of strong floral aromas such as those of dried rose petals. It is made as a dry, off-dry, sweet, or very sweet wine. In all versions, Gewürztraminer leaves a nip of bitterness in its aftertaste.

Merlot (mer-LOH)

Softer and fleshier than Cabernet Sauvignon, Merlot also tends to be less acidic. When it is the major grape or the only grape in a red wine, it matures sooner than a Cabernet Sauvignon. Wines made from this grape are easier to drink when they are young. Serve Merlot wines with richer, more substantial foods.

Pinot Gris (PEE-noh GREE)

Pinot Gris grapes make a full-bodied, sturdy white wine that is often a bit low in acidity. It has an assertive, spicy aroma.

Pinot Blanc (PEE-noh BLAHNGK)

If you like white wines made with Chardonnay grapes, you probably will like wines made from Pinot Blanc grapes as well. Although subtler, usually firmer, and slightly more tart, Pinot Blanc wines are closely related in taste and aroma to Chardonnay.

Pinot Noir (PEE-noh NWAHR)

One of the world's greatest grapes, Pinot Noir produces glorious red wines. Some of these are Musigny (moos-een-ye), Corton (cor-tawn),

Romanée-Conti (ro-ma-nay CAWN-tee), Volnay (vawl-nay), and Pommard (po-MAR). All red Burgundies are made entirely of Pinot Noir. The best Pinot Noirs are wines of incomparable depth and harmony. The aromas of Pinot Noir wines have been described as similar to violets, cherries, leather, peppermint, or truffles. The textures of Pinot Noir wines have been described as satin and velvet.

Riesling (REEZ-ling)

If you like a balance of sweetness and acidity, Riesling white wines are for you. Riesling has an aroma of fresh flowers when a young wine, and a subtler perfume as it matures. Riesling can be dry or it can produce some of the world's greatest naturally sweet wines, strong in apricot and peachlike scents, and also as rich as nectar.

Sauvignon Blanc (SOH-vihn-yohn BLAHNGK)

This is an important white grape in France, where it is blended with semillon grapes to produce all Bordeaux's (bohr-DOH) white wines—from dry Graves (GRAHV) to sweet dessert wines of Sauternes (soh-TEHRN). It is also the grape of Sancerre (sawn-sair) wine and Pouilly Fumé (poo-YE fyoo-may) wine in the eastern Loire Valley of France. In California, this wine is also labeled Fumé Blanc (fyoo-may BLAHNGK).

Syrah (see-rah)

This grape makes a deep-colored red wine, rough, highly acidic and peppery in its young days, yet it can mature to a big, velvety wine.

Zinfandel (ZIHN-fuhn-dehl)

Zinfandel grapes are very versatile, and as a result they are the most widely planted red grape in California. All types of wines have been made from it, from fruity young wines to fine table wines, heavy port-like wines and the currently popular blush wines. Beef Wellington with Cumberland Sauce is a great choice to serve with a Zinfandel wine.

13 Table Conversation

Your guests have been seated. The before-dinner drinks have been served. Dinner has been ordered. What do you do now? It's your job as the host to get the conversation rolling, regulate it, keep it rolling, and change topics if necessary. Where do you begin? Starting and maintaining a conversation involve not only knowing what to say and when to say it, but also knowing what not to say and when to keep quiet.

ESSENTIAL SKILLS

A good conversationalist has many qualities. She is knowledgeable about a variety of topics, has a sense of humor that enables her to entertain others, and she can laugh at herself. She has many interests and is able to vary conversation topics to fit the person or audience she is speaking to. A good conversationalist never talks down to her listeners. She is also a very good listener and is truly interested in what others have to say. This is perhaps the most important quality of all; the ability to listen to others even when we're bored or uninterested is the greatest skill we can develop. Listen attentively to all information.

It will amaze you how many times it will be information you will need in the future. Being able to talk about a variety of topics, being sensitive to others, having an assortment of interests, and carefully listening to what others are saying and are interested in will all enable you to come up with many appropriate dinner table conversation topics.

YOUR AUDIENCE

Consider your guests, clients, or audience. If you're discussing business over dinner with colleagues, then you may need to make small talk and discuss trivial matters for about a half an hour before business dominates the remainder of the conversation. If business is the reason for the hour-long lunch, then stick to business. There will be very little time to discuss anything else.

The conversations at dinner parties in people's homes and at restaurants vary widely, depending upon the nature of the guests and the reason for the dinner. One good place to start is to think of common interests. If the other guests are people you see occasionally or associate with regularly, you can ask about recent developments in their lives or about what they've been doing since you last spoke. If you're going to be meeting many people at the dinner for the first time, get ready to make small talk.

SMALL TALK SUBJECTS

Small talk can be a lifesaver in many situations. It fills the voids in conversations, helps ease tense moments, sets others at ease, and helps us become acquainted with others. There are two ways to make initiating small talk a little easier. The first is to be well informed, as all good conversationalists are. This means being able to discuss topics such as current best-selling books, news events, famous people, fitness crazes, medical and technological advances, travel, and sports. These are all appropriate small talk subjects.

The second way to ease into small talk is by asking others about themselves, their family, work, or hobby. If you know one of your guests or the host is particularly knowledgeable about wines or has wines as a hobby, you might steer conversation to that area. For example, you might ask your guest if white wine can be made from red grapes. "Yes, it can be. The wine is made without the skin of the grapes. It is the skin of the red grapes that gives the wine its red color."

Another question you could ask is, "Are inexpensive wines the most sugary?" The answer is yes and no. Yes, the cheapest wines are more sugary, but so are the most expensive wines.

CONVERSATION STOPPERS

Asking a person generally about himself is acceptable. However, asking someone very personal or intimate questions, such as inquiries into his religious beliefs, financial situation, terminal illness or any illness, or personal details about a divorce or an affair, are strictly off limits. Neither should one ask about someone's weight, height or shoe size, or about age or mental health. Exceptions are people who are best friends or who are absolutely comfortable discussing these subjects with one another.

Spreading gossip that is harmful to others, and telling racial, ethnic and sexually oriented jokes should be avoided. You never know who's going to be offended by them even if they don't admit it or show it. Avoid issues that have been overly discussed and are no longer interesting to the majority of people.

Conversation does not need to include the fact that you just received your big bonus at work or that last night you picked up the adorable blouse you're wearing for only $29.95. Leave money matters at home. Your dinner companion may not want to enlighten you about his Uncle Wally's bankruptcy hearing, so don't ask about it. Unless they bring it up first, avoid asking about or discussing your guest's or host's misfortunes.

Don't bring up strongly debatable and controversial issues such as abortion, women's rights, the rights of homosexuals, and so forth, if you don't know how the other person feels about them. Getting into a detailed discussion about a person's health or illnesses is also very inconsiderate. It's fine to ask how a person is, but don't call attention to another's disease or state of being, and if someone asks about your health, don't tell them about every little ache and pain you have. Keep your answer short and general.

RESPONSES TO RUDENESS

If you are asked a rude question or are the recipient of a tactless comment, you have every right not to respond to or acknowledge the question or comment. You may wish to reply in a very vague manner or give them no answer at all and hope the person gets the hint. It's also acceptable simply to say that you don't want to discuss an issue.

MONITORING CONVERSATIONS

Your job as the host includes mediating conversations if the need arises; knowing when to switch to a lighter topic, when to end the chitchat and get on to business; making sure everyone is introduced to everyone else; and making sure that everyone is involved in conversation. You don't want to leave one or two people out of a conversation because they are shy or unfamiliar with the topic being discussed. Include them in a conversation by starting it with something you know they are involved or interested in.

With the close proximity of tables in many restaurants today, check around to see who is near. Confidentiality is important. It is wise not to discuss anything that may be even slightly confidential when dining out in a restaurant. Also, be conscious of your voice level and speak softly.

14 Coping with Tableware

How do you choose from the variety of silverware in front of you? Again, it's not as difficult as it may look. There should be no more than three of each type of utensil beside your plate. You simply start from the outside and work your way in, using one utensil per course. Your salad fork is on your outermost left, followed by your dinner fork. Your soup spoon is on your outermost right, followed by your salad knife and dinner knife. Your dessert spoon and fork are above your plate. If you follow this simple rule of working from the outside in, you'll have the correct utensils for each course. If you're still unsure about which fork or spoon to use, follow the lead of your host, since she will be the first to eat. Rest your utensils across the edge of a plate, tines up, not on the tablecloth, when you are finished with them. Return serving forks to the platter with the tines down.

Forks . . . Which One to Use

Do you use your fork as a shovel to fill your mouth with food as fast as you can? Or do you wrap your hand around your fork and hold onto it as if it is made of pure silver? Or maybe you are a track-and-field fan and spear your food with your fork as if it is a javelin? If any of these descriptions matches your behavior, read on, because not only is it important to know which fork to use with each course, it's equally important to know how to use each fork correctly.

Whether it's a dinner, salad, seafood, or dessert fork you're struggling with, the accepted way to hold them is the same for all. Learn how to hold one, and you've mastered holding them all. The fork is not a utensil to be used as a shovel, gripped and held onto for dear life, or to be thrown like a javelin or spear. Forks are properly held delicately, at a slight angle and between the thumb, forefinger, and middle finger, with the tines up. Keep your fingers away from the tines.

The dinner fork is the largest fork by your plate and is usually placed immediately to the left of the plate. Use it to eat vegetables and meat. It also can be used to eat salad and fish if salad and fish forks aren't provided. Taking butter from the butter plate and putting it on your vegetables is also done with your dinner fork. When not using your dinner fork or when finished eating, rest it tines up, on your dinner plate, not on the tablecloth.

The salad fork is most obviously used for eating salad. It is also acceptable to use it to eat fish, first courses, and luncheons with it if other forks aren't provided. Where this fork is placed on the table depends upon how it will be used. If the salad will be served before the entrée (as is most common in the United States), it is placed to the left of the dinner fork. If the salad follows the main course, the salad fork is placed to the right of the dinner fork. If fish will be the first course and the salad fork is to be used, this fork is placed to the left of the dinner fork. At a luncheon, the salad fork will be the major fork in the place setting if it is to be used as the luncheon fork. If the salad fork is above the plate, to the right of the dinner fork, or to the right of another salad fork, use it as a dessert fork. Hold the salad fork the same way you'd hold a dinner fork and place it tines up on the plate after use.

Seafood such as clams, lobster, and oysters are often difficult enough to eat as it is, but using the wrong fork can make the situation even worse. That is when seafood forks are helpful. Held the same as a dinner fork, these smaller forks make removing the meat from shells much easier. The seafood fork can be found on either the outermost right or to the left of the plate. The proper resting place for this fork when you are finished is tines up on the plate on which the seafood was served.

People often associate using spoons, not forks, with eating dessert, but there are some foods that are easier eaten with a fork. It's really a matter of personal preference or using whichever utensil works best for you for the food you're eating. The dessert fork may be found in a variety of places. It may be presented with the dessert, it may be immediately to the left of the plate, or it may be above the dinner plate. This fork is also held the same way a dinner fork is and is rested on the dessert plate, tines up, after use.

Fish forks are held like dinner forks. However, this fork has broader tines and works well for picking bones out of meat. A salad fork may also be used for this purpose. The fish fork is placed tines up on the plate when you are finished, to safeguard against having the fork drop off the plate.

KNIVES AND MEAT CUTTING

Contrary to how you may have to sometimes use them, as when you get an especially tough piece of meat, knives are not saws. Knives, like forks, are properly held gently but firmly. They're held in the hand with the thumb, middle, ring, and pinky fingers surrounding the handle. The forefinger is placed on the top edge of the blade, near the handle, not toward the tip, to provide pressure and stabilize the knife.

All knives except the butter knife need to be placed on the edge of your plate, with the cutting edge facing you when not in use. If you have a butter knife, it rests on the edge of the butter plate.

Along with your dinner fork, you have your dinner knife. The dinner knife is the largest knife by your plate. It is used to cut meat, vegetables, and anything else on the dinner plate. It also can be used to cut your salad if the leaves are too large to fit into your mouth. When you do not have a butter knife, which is most of the time these days, use the dinner knife while it is still clean as your butter knife. The dinner knife is the one closest to the plate on the right side. The cutting edge of the blade always faces the plate.

The steak knife is held the same way as the dinner knife. It is the knife to the right of the dinner knife. This is also where the fish knife can be found, but you can easily distinguish between the two. The steak knife has a serrated edge and a pointed tip, whereas the fish knife has an unusual shape and a smooth edge. Also, if your meal consists of steak and not fish or vice versa, your place setting will include only one knife, not both.

You will sometimes find a butter knife both on the butter plate and alongside your plate. The butter knife resting on the butter plate is used to place a pat of butter on your bread and butter or dinner plate. The butter knife by your plate is then used to butter your bread. Don't butter the whole piece of bread or roll all at once; break off and butter a few mouthfuls before eating them.

The fish knife has a unique shape that is designed to cut around fish bones. This knife is held with the notched edge up. The smooth, curved edge is held down to cut the meat. Hold the knife between your thumb and middle finger where the blade meets the handle. Rest your forefinger on the notched edge near the handle for pressure and support.

There are two ways to use a dinner or steak knife with a fork to cut and eat meat. One is the American style. Cut the meat by holding the knife in your right hand while holding the meat to your plate by having your fork, tines in the meat, in your left hand. Cut two or three bite-sized pieces of meat, then lay your knife across the top edge of your plate with the sharp side of the blade facing in. Put your fork in your right hand to eat.

The other style of cutting and eating meat is the European or Continental style. This is most commonly used in Europe, but it is also used widely in Canada and in some parts of the United States. This style is the same as the American in that you cut your meat by holding your knife in your right hand while securing your food with your fork in your left hand. Instead of placing the knife along the top of the plate and switching your fork to your right hand, simply eat the cut pieces of food by picking them up with your fork still in your left hand. Hold your knife in your right hand throughout the meal.

With either style, you can use your knife to push small pieces of food such as peas or corn onto your fork. Both styles are acceptable. Still, check out the culture or environment you are in and choose the style that is the most natural and comfortable for you.

SPOONS . . . ALL EIGHT OF THEM

If you thought there were many knives and forks to keep straight, hold onto your chair: There are eight different kinds of spoons. But don't worry. Just as the knives and forks all have their purposes, so do the spoons. And you probably won't ever have to deal with more than three spoons at one place setting. One nice factor about this multitude of spoons is that they're all held the same way. Spoons are correctly held between the thumb and forefinger at the midpoint of the handle. They too need to be held gently but firmly and not used as a shovel or held in your fist.

Dinner spoons are becoming spoons of the past. Most sets of silverware have replaced them with teaspoons, but some older sets have them. It's more convenient to eat foods such as cereals, soups, and desserts with dinner spoons because they are bigger than teaspoons. If your place setting includes a dinner spoon, it is found on the right side of your knife.

If there isn't a dinner spoon, the teaspoon is to the right of your knife. This spoon is used to eat a variety of foods, including cereal, and to stir coffee and tea. You will find a teaspoon next to your plate even if you don't need it, because, with your knife and fork, it completes your place setting.

Don't be confused if you encounter two different-sized soup spoons. If you're having a thick soup that will be served in a bowl, you'll use a larger soup spoon than you would if you ordered consommé. Regardless of the spoon you use, place a used spoon either on the plate under the bowl or in the bowl or cup if there is no plate underneath. It is not acceptable to place it on the tablecloth or on your dinner plate.

You'll know a grapefruit spoon when you see one. It has serrated edges leading up to the point. This makes it easier to dig the sections out of the rind. If a grapefruit spoon isn't provided, it's acceptable to use a teaspoon.

You will find your dessert spoon above your dinner plate, alongside the plate next to your knife, or presented with your dessert. It often has a longer and narrower bowl than the other spoons. After eating your dessert, place your dessert spoon on your dessert plate.

An iced tea spoon is a great spoon not only for iced tea but also for root beer floats, ice cream sundaes, and malts or shakes. It works well for eating these items because of its long handle and small bowl. You will receive this spoon when you order iced tea, a float, or a sundae.

Would you like an espresso? If so, you'll receive a demitasse spoon with it. This is a tiny spoon made expressly for stirring espresso. It is served with your espresso and rests on the plate underneath the cup when you are finished.

PLATES AND PLACE SETTINGS

You knew something was wrong when your cherry tomato rolled off the plate. You had hardly any salad on your salad plate, but it was already full. And when it came time for the bread and butter, why did your bread plate seem as if it was there to hold half a loaf of bread instead of just the slice and pat of butter that you had on it? I'm sure you figured out by then you had mistaken your salad plate for your bread and butter plate and vice versa. People are sometimes just as confused about which plates to use for the different courses as they are about which silverware to use. Fortunately though, keeping your plates straight is probably even easier than struggling with the silverware.

You will find your salad plate in one of two places, either to the left of your napkin or on top of your dinner plate in the middle of the place setting. The salad plate is smaller than the dinner plate but larger than the bread and butter plate. To save table space at large pre-set banquet tables you will often find your salad plate above your forks. If you're dining in a restaurant and your salad plate is on top of your dinner plate, you may place the salad plate to the left of the dinner plate if you want to eat your salad with or after your entrée. If you are at a dinner party in someone's home, leave the salad plate where the host placed it.

The bread and butter plate is placed to the left of the dinner plate above the forks. It is the smallest plate in the setting, other than the saucer under the coffee cup. Today it is rare for all but the finest restaurants to provide a butter knife. However, if there is a butter knife you will find it lying across the top of the bread and butter plate. This is one way to easily distinguish it from your salad plate if you can't remember which one goes where. It's also acceptable to place other small finger foods, such as raw vegetables or olives, on the bread and butter plate. If there isn't a bread and butter plate at your setting, place your bread on your dinner plate.

Other plates that you need to be aware of are the dinner/luncheon plate, the service plate, the dessert plate, and the cup and saucer. The dinner/luncheon plate is the largest plate in the setting and is found in the middle of the place setting. Dinner plates are larger than luncheon plates, and the one in your place setting is determined by whether you are eating dinner or lunch. Your place setting will have one or the other, not both. The entrée, vegetables, and salad, if a salad plate isn't provided, are all eaten from this plate.

The service plate often serves as a salad or luncheon plate as well. You will most often find the service plate on top of your dinner plate. It is used to hold appetizers and soup bowls and is removed after these courses. If appetizers and soup aren't included in the meal, the service plate is removed before the entrée is served. If a salad plate isn't in the place setting, it's acceptable to use the service plate. If this plate is used as a luncheon plate, it will be the main plate in the center of the place setting.

Upon completion of the entrée, the dinner plate is removed and replaced by the dessert plate. This plate is placed in the center of the place setting before dessert is served or at the time the dessert is served if it's served directly on the dessert plate. Like the dinner plate, the dessert plate remains in the center of the place setting when you are finished.

The cup and saucer are found to the far right of the place setting. They are placed in line horizontally with the salad plate on the far left and the dinner plate in the center of the place setting. Only when you are dining casually and only after the table has been cleared is it acceptable to move your cup and saucer to the center of the place setting.

The correct way to hold a cup is to grasp the handle with your thumb and index finger, and to rest your next finger under the handle. There is no need to put your thumb or finger through the hole.

A table for left-handed people is set the same way as a table for right-handed people. Unfortunately for left-handers, they can't rearrange the place setting. They can use their silverware in the way that is most comfortable for them, however. Because the server will be removing the plate from the right, left-handed people should leave their silverware on the right-hand side of their plate, just as right-handed people do, so it doesn't fall off.

(More information about tableware and all the basics about setting a proper table can be found in Table Setting Guide, from Brighton Publications, Inc.)

15 Eating Food Gracefully

What do apples, french fries, lobster, corn on the cob, spaghetti, fish, and watermelon all have in common? All can be difficult to eat neatly. You know how you'd eat them at home. Yet, is it okay to use the same techniques when you're eating these foods in a restaurant? Some of them, yes. Others, probably not.

You will probably want to carefully choose what to order when you are dining out for business. You probably won't want to order a whole lobster unless you're in a restaurant known for it. Instead, consider ordering things that are easy to eat.

Apples and pears — These fruits are to be served quartered and cored. They may be peeled or unpeeled. The quarters can be eaten with the fingers or cut with a knife and eaten with a fork.

Artichokes — Artichokes are a definite finger food. The leaves are pulled off one at a time and the pulpy part is dipped into the sauce provided. The pulpy base is then scraped off the leaf with your teeth. Place the leaves on the side of your plate or on another plate if one has been provided for this purpose. Use your knife to scrape away the choke, the abrasive, prickly part surrounding the heart. Eat the heart with your fork and knife.

Asparagus — Personal preference is the deciding factor when eating asparagus. It can be eaten with the fingers, but if it starts getting too stringy as you work your way down the stem, cut it with a knife and eat it with your fork. Leave the tough, uneaten portion on your plate.

Avocado — Eat a sliced avocado with a fork. Use a spoon to dig it out of a halved shell.

Bacon — It's not a good idea to cut crisp bacon with a fork or knife or eat it with a fork unless you want to send it flying onto someone else's plate. Crisp bacon is most easily eaten with your fingers. If it's not cooked to a crisp, use your knife and fork.

Bottled drinks and carbonated beverages — The best way to consume these beverages is to drink them from a glass. Your second option is to drink them from a bottle with a straw. Avoid drinking from the bottle.

Bread and butter — Place a piece of bread and butter on your bread plate, and then pass the bread basket to your right. Tear off a small piece of bread or break the roll in half, butter it, and eat. Bread shouldn't be eaten in whole slices unless it's toast or garlic bread.

Cake — Whether it's birthday cake, wedding cake, or your favorite chocolate cake that your mom made especially for you, use your fork to eat it. Only hard or solid cakes, such as fruitcake, should be eaten with the fingers.

Cheese — The way cheese is served determines how it is to be eaten. Use your knife to spread it on crackers if it's served as hors d'oeuvres or if it's a soft cheese. If served as a dessert with fruit, use your fork to cut and eat it.

Clams, fried — Fried clams are best eaten with your fingers.

Clams, steamed — With your fingers, hold the clam by its neck to remove it from its shell. Dip it into the clam broth, then the butter sauce, then eat it whole. You may drink the broth when you are finished dipping the clams.

Corn on the cob — What goes best with fried chicken and barbecues? Corn on the cob of course! Cutting the kernels off the cob isn't generally acceptable, so even that is not a viable solution. Breaking the cob in half may make things a little easier. You can butter and salt the whole cob at once or just do enough for two or three bites, whichever is neatest for you. Eating across the cob or around it is a matter of personal preference; either is acceptable.

Eggs — Hard-cooked eggs are a finger food. Just break the shell with a knife, peel, and eat. Soft-cooked eggs are to be eaten from the shell with a teaspoon. All other varieties are eaten with a fork.

Escargot (snails) — If served in the shell, tongs and a small fork are provided. The tongs are held in the left hand if you're right-handed, and vice versa. The shell is held in the tongs, and the snail is removed using the small fork.

Fish — If you receive a fish that is served whole and you're not sure how to filet it, you may ask the waiter to do it for you. Otherwise, remove the head and tail (optional) and cut down the length of the fish along the upper edge. Lift the top filet away from the backbone. Use your knife and fork to remove the entire skeleton, and set it on the side of your plate. The meat can be eaten using your fork and knife or only your fork. There may still be small bones in the meat. If you get one in your mouth, remove it with your thumb and forefinger.

French fries — When having french fries with finger foods such as hot dogs and sandwiches, eat them with your fingers. When eating french fries with other foods, cut and eat them with a fork.

Fried or barbecued chicken — Just the idea of it may make you a little chicken to eat it, but it's really not too difficult. Picking it up and eating it with your fingers is okay on only three occasions: if you're eating it at home, if it's served in a basket, or if it's served at a barbecue. If dining at a restaurant or at a dinner party, use your knife and fork. If others start using their fingers or if you get the host's approval, then you may eat it with your fingers.

Game birds and frogs legs — At formal meals, using your fork and knife to remove meat from the bones and to disjoint the legs and wings is the only acceptable way to eat these meats. At more casual affairs, you may pick up the bones with your fingers after you have removed as much meat as possible and have disjointed the legs and wings using your knife and fork.

Garnishes — Carrots, cherry tomatoes, parsley, watercress, radishes, pickles, and olives are all finger foods.

Grapefruit — Grapefruit is normally served halved with the sections cut so the fruit may be removed using a grapefruit spoon. Picking it up to squeeze out the juice is a no-no. If grapefruit is served whole, it can be peeled and sectioned just as an orange would be.

Grapes — A single grape should not be pulled from a bunch in a serving bowl. The correct way to eat them is to break or cut a stem of grapes off the bunch. Then individual grapes are pulled off. If the grapes have seeds, spit them into your hand and then put them on your plate.

Gravy — If you use gravy, pour it gradually over your meat, but don't drown it. If you like to sponge up gravy with bread, break the bread into small chunks and put it in the gravy. Then eat it using your fork.

Hard-shelled crabs — Using your fingers, remove the legs, and attracting as little attention as possible, suck the meat from the legs. To pick out the body meat, place the body on its back and use an oyster fork or nut pick to remove it. Use a nutcracker to crack the claws.

Ice cream — Take a small enough portion of ice cream in your spoon so that it can all be eaten in one bite.

Kiwi — New Zealanders eat their kiwis unpeeled. They cut them in half and eat them with a small spoon. Another way to eat kiwis is peeled, cut in half, and eaten with a small fork. Or you can peel and slice kiwis.

Lemons — Use caution when squeezing lemons; you don't want to squirt yourself or anyone else. Hold your hand over and around the lemon as you squeeze or shield the lemon with your spoon to prevent the juice from hitting someone.

Lobster — In finer restaurants, lobster may be served already cracked. But it's probably a good idea to brush up on your lobster-eating skills anyway. Begin by twisting off the front claws, cracking them, and removing the meat with an oyster fork or nut pick. A fork can be used to remove the tail meat after the tail has been broken off. The tail meat can be cut up with a fork and knife. If your lobster tail has green roe at the end of the tail meat, it may be eaten. This green roe, which is lobster eggs, is found only in female lobsters. Some people think it is a delicacy. If you prefer not to eat it, scrape it off, and push it aside with your fork. Break off the legs and suck the meat out of them. Forget it if you're full. The legs have little meat in them, and mainly water.

Mangoes — Quarter and peel a mango while securing it on the plate with a fork. Cut the quarters and eat the pieces with a spoon or fork.

Melons — If served as balls, eat with a spoon. If halved, quartered, or cut into wedges and served in the rind, use a spoon to scrape the melon out. Cut and eat peeled and quartered melons with your fork.

Mussels — If you can suck mussels from the shell without spilling the sauce or juice or making any embarrassing noises, this is an acceptable way to eat them. If you're not quite so neat, your best bet is to use a fork to pick them out of the shells. You can sip the juice out of the shell by raising it to your lips. Broth accompanying the mussels should be eaten with a spoon.

Oranges — Use a knife to peel the orange and then break the sections apart. Eat one section at a time. If an orange is served cut in half, eat it as you would a grapefruit—one section at a time. Oranges that are peeled and cut in half can be cut with a knife and eaten with a fork.

Oysters (and clams on the half shell) — Remove the meat with a fork while holding the shell in the other hand. After dipping it in sauce, swallow it whole.

Papayas — Cut in half and eat with a spoon.

Pie — When served à la mode, eat pie with a spoon and a fork. Eat all other varieties with a fork. Start from the point and work toward the crust.

Pineapple chunks — Eat pineapple chunks with a fork.

Pizza — The only time you might not want to eat pizza with your fingers is when you're in a restaurant. Even then, all you really need to do is use your fork for the first few bites.

Potato chips — There is no better way to eat potato chips than with your fingers.

Salad — Lettuce leaves, vegetable pieces, and chunks of meat must be cut if they're too big to fit into your mouth. Cutting your entire salad at once is not recommended, though.

Sandwiches — Using a knife and fork is the safest way to eat a sandwich if it's very big or messy. Otherwise, use your hands.

Shrimp — If shrimp is in the shell, carefully remove the shell by holding the legs in your fingers and peeling the shell around and off. Hold the shrimp by the tail and dip it in the sauce. Businesspeople think that this is one time that using your fingers to hold the tail and dip it in the sauce makes the most sense. Otherwise you have to keep wiping off your hands as you switch from peeling to using your fork for dipping. However, it is acceptable to use your fork, spear a shrimp, dip it into the sauce and eat it. This is the method you may prefer when the shrimp has already been cleaned and shelled before serving. Shells are to be left in the cocktail bowl or on your bread and butter plate.

Soup — Spoon soup away from you. Lean forward, but don't hunch over when bringing the soup to your mouth. Quietly sip soup from the side of the spoon, not from the tip. Between sips the spoon is put on the underplate. A spoon should not be left in a soup cup at any time. You may drink only thin soup from a bowl, and only if the bowl has handles. Still, take a few spoonfuls first. Thick soups or soups containing pieces of vegetables or meat are always to be eaten with a spoon. When tipping a bowl to get the last few drops of soup, tip the bowl away from you. Soup au gratin can be very difficult to eat because the cheese is often stringy or clumps together. Order this only if you're sure you can eat it gracefully. When you're finished, your soup spoon is to be placed on the right side of the underplate or as a last resort, leave the spoon in the soup bowl if there is no underplate.

Spaghetti — Twirling spaghetti around your fork and then putting it in your mouth is the best method. You also can twirl the spaghetti into a spoon if one is provided. It is not acceptable to put one end of a noodle in your mouth and suck the rest in.

Stewed fruits — Eat with a spoon or fork.

16 Tips on Tipping

Whether you call it a "gratuity" and think of it as a present, or you call it a "tip" to ensure promptness, the result is the same. You give someone money above and beyond what you owe them for the services they've provided. How much you tip is purely a personal matter, and completely up to you. Usually, however, the tip you leave needs to be between 15 and 20 percent of the total bill. If the service was exceptional, leave more if you desire. If the service was poor, leaving less provides the person with a wealth of information about his performance. Leaving a small tip is recommended even if the service was extremely poor, because many people need tips to supplement their typically minimum wage. In such a case, though, you should notify the manager of the poor quality of service you received, so he can prevent it from happening to others. You will be safe in almost every situation if you tip 15 to 20 percent of the tab, but remember that tipping rules aren't written in stone. Consider the quality of the service and the finished product before deciding how much to tip. The following are recommended amounts to tip various service providers.

No Tipping Necessary

We'll start with the easy ones—those you don't need to tip. This category includes buspersons, chefs, owners and managers of establishments, musicians, doctors, dentists, sports pros, and other professionals. Complimenting chefs on a well-prepared meal and owners and managers on their establishment is appreciated. If you want to tip a musician, give no less than $5.

HOTELS

You may not realize it, but there are many hotel employees who serve you during your stay there. Remember to tip each accordingly. The attendant who carries your bags to your room should receive a dollar per bag, $3 or $4 if you brought many clothes. If she opens your door, turns on the lights, and otherwise makes you feel at home, include a little extra. Your housekeeper deserves $1 a night for stays longer than one night, more if your room looks like a tornado hit it. The valet receives $1 to $2 for bringing your car to you. And 50¢ to $1 is an acceptable tip for the door attendant who calls you a cab.

THE CONCIERGE

You typically find a concierge in finer hotels only, but probably will wish that all hotels had them because of the many services he provides. Many hotels provide concierge services at no charge. At other hotels you receive a bill from the concierge after your stay, but this doesn't excuse you from tipping him $2 to $10 for each service he provides or leaving $5 to $50 total at the end of your stay. Services a concierge may provide include arranging for a babysitter, getting theater tickets, and making restaurant, taxi, and airline reservations. Base the amount of each tip or your final tip on how much the concierge did for you, and whether you'd like to receive the same treatment if you stay at that hotel again.

RESTAURANTS

In most restaurants, tipping the server 15 to 20 percent of the bill, including drinks but not sales tax, is sufficient. If there is a coat room, the attendant should receive 50¢ to 75¢ per coat.

In fine, expensive restaurants, a tip of 20 percent of the total bill is recommended. Seventy-five percent of this goes to the server, the other 25 to the captain. The wine steward receives a tip of $3 to $5 per bottle, or 15 percent of the wine bill if you're in a very expensive restaurant. The rest room, coat room, and door attendant are tipped $1 per person, coat, and car, respectively. A garage attendant receives $1 or $2 for bringing your car to the door.

Customers who are regulars at a restaurant usually tip the maitre d' $10 every four or five visits. If you're new to a particular restaurant, tipping the maitre d' $20 may make a difference in the service you receive. Tip the maitre d' by giving him money in a handshake. A bartender receives 15 percent of your drink bill if you have had a few beverages in the bar before your meal.

If you're paying by credit card, write in the amount of your tip, based on your total bill, in the blank space provided for it on the bill. It's also acceptable to leave currency on the table as the tip, and just pay for your meal only with your credit card. Servers often appreciate this, as they receive their tip right then. Restaurants and servers actually prefer that you do this rather than add the tip to the bill, because 2 to 3 percent of the bill goes to the credit card company as part of their service charge.

Delivery People

Isn't saving you from having to drive in a snow or rainstorm worth a dollar or two? Not to mention the convenience of having someone bring your lunch or dinner right to your office.? Gratuities are usually not included in the cost of the food that you are having delivered. Delivery people are often using their own cars, and it takes time to make personal deliveries. Consider your driver's effort. Most delivery people deserve a tip of at least 15 to 20 percent. For those who deliver groceries, give $1 to $5, depending on how many grocery bags they delivered.

Caterers' Employees

Before you tip your caterer's employees, ask if a tip is already included in the bill. If it is, it will usually be figured at a rate of 15 percent. If not, you should tip the head server 15 to 20 percent of the bill (sound familiar?), letting him know that it is to be divided among the rest of the staff. If you required only the services of a bartender and one or two servers, the tip to be divided among them may be handed to the individual who presents the bill, or they may be tipped individually. It is never necessary for guests to tip the catering staff.

TAXI DRIVERS

If your cab driver took you directly where you wanted to go without showing you the whole town first or otherwise gave you satisfactory service, tip her 15 to 20 percent of the fare. If she is totally uncooperative and you were scared for your life, no tip is necessary.

HIRED DRIVERS

When you hit the town in style by renting a limo, expect to tip the driver at least 15 percent of rental cost. You're not expected to tip drivers of air-travel limousines, though.

CADDIES

Show your caddie just how much you appreciate his lugging your golf bag around the course by remembering to tip him. A tip of 20 to 25 percent of the fee after the game isn't too much. It's also acceptable to give the tip to the caddie master later, specifying which caddie you had, if you've left your wallet in the locker room or car.

TOWEL ATTENDANTS

After a workout or a brisk game of racquetball, remember to tip the towel attendant. Fifty cents to $1 is appropriate if he brings you a towel. If you request any toiletries, the tip increases to $2.

SHIPS

The amount to tip a ship's crew varies from ship to ship. The best way to find out how much you should tip for your particular ship is to get recommendations from the ship's purser or cruise director. They usually are sure to let you know this, so you don't even have to ask. Gratuities are customarily given the last evening of your cruise. Some general gratuities guidelines are as follows: Tip more if you're staying in an expensive room. The cabin and stateroom (dining room) steward are tipped $3 per person per day, $5 on luxurious ships and in more expensive rooms. The busperson receives $1.50 per person per day. Remember the "per day" part of these recommendations. Believe me, they don't want you to forget.

Other personnel, such as wine stewards, bar waiters, attendants, and deck stewards may be tipped as service is rendered. The suggested gratuity is 15 percent of the bill. Fifteen to 20 percent of each bar bill is given to the bar and lounge stewards. If you're traveling with lots of luggage, expect to tip the porters accordingly. Five dollars isn't unreasonable. Tip your maitre d' and head server at your discretion.

TRAINS

Because traveling by train isn't as common as it once was, it's not surprising that many people are unsure of whom and how much to tip when they find themselves having to take an overnight journey on a train. There are several staff members on a train who should be tipped for their services. One is the club car attendant, who gets 15 percent of the tab. Another is the porter, who receives $1 per day. The Pullman porter is tipped several dollars a day. Finally, the server receives 15 to 20 percent of the dining bill.

GUIDES

Nothing can ruin a vacation or trip quite like getting lost. Unless you enjoy driving around for hours without having the slightest idea of where you're going, a guide is usually well worth hiring and tipping. Hunting guides receive 10 percent of the fee, but you may want to give more if you bring home the "big one." Ten to 20 percent of a tour cost is an appropriate tip for a tour guide. There is still no need to tip government guides.

17 Hiring a Caterer

If you've never hired a caterer before, you may think all there is to it is simply selecting one from the phone book. But, once you know more about the process of hiring a caterer, you're probably going to want to put a little more effort into it.

WHEN SHOULD YOU HIRE A CATERER?

The first step is to know when you really need to hire a caterer:

◄ When you're planning on 25 or more guests.

◄ When your menu includes a variety of exotic foods, or foods that are most successfully prepared by a professional.

◄ When you don't have access to cooking facilities where you can prepare the large amount of food you'll need.

◄ When the event is held in a public center or hall.

◄ When the host can't physically prepare the food.

◄ When the event doesn't take place in the host's town or in one nearby, and she will be arriving in the area only a short time before the event.

◄ When the event is impromptu.

SERVICES TO EXPECT

Now that you've decided that you need to hire a caterer, how do you go about selecting one? The first thing you need to know is that not all caterers provide the same services. At one extreme, some do nothing more than cook your meal for you. At the other extreme, some do everything for you, including cleanup afterward. This allows you to relax beforehand, enjoy your party, and relax afterward. Matching a caterer's services to your needs will not only result in less frustration on your part, but will also help you stay within your budget.

The caterer you hire may prepare all the food in her kitchen, prepare it in yours, or do a little of both. She may provide all the ingredients, beverages, bartenders, dishes, silverware, and servers, or it may be necessary for you to provide some of them. Buying the beverages (alcoholic and nonalcoholic) yourself can save you money. Because not all caterers provide them, you may have to hire bartenders and servers separately. Some serve only a few for a sit-down dinner; others cater for large events. Some caterers adapt their services even to the most imaginative of party environments—tents, cruise ships, corporate jets. Again, you may want to shop around to find the caterer who'll best meet your needs.

The most reliable method is to hire one whose food you've eaten or whose services you've experienced at another event. Chances are that if you were satisfied with her expertise and the services she provided for someone else, you'll be equally happy with the job she does for you. Another way to find a good caterer is to ask around. Word of mouth and a caterer's reputation are your best alternatives if you haven't witnessed a caterer's performance yourself. It's always a good idea to call two or three caterers who are recommended to you and ask for price estimates. Also ask for references from clients who have hosted events similar to yours. There shouldn't be much difference between the prices of caterers if they all provide approximately the same services. A prompt and professionally presented estimate signals a good caterer. Also, hiring a caterer who has a regular, experienced staff may save you money and prevent headaches. Other topics you need to discuss during this call are:

◄ the date

◄ the place

◄ the size and nature of your party

◄ your budget

◄ decorating ideas.

After selecting the caterer who's right for you and booking him as far in advance as possible, it's time to get down to the details. Here are some points to consider and questions to ask:

◄ Are you going to plan the menu or leave it to his discretion?

◄ Where will the meal be prepared?

◄ Will he prepare all the food, or are you going to prepare certain items?

◄ Will he discuss the quality of the food used?

◄ What size portion will the guests receive?

◄ Has he ever catered before at the site at which your event will take place?

◄ Is he going to provide all the dishes, tables, chairs, linen, serving platters, and so on, or do you have to provide some of these items? What is the quality of the items that he provides? What condition are they in and how old is the caterer's serving equipment?

◄ If the caterer is providing these items, is this service included in the charge per guest? What is the charge per guest?

◄ Will he break down all costs for you and provide a written estimate of all costs?

◄ What other equipment will you need to provide? Will you receive a discount if you supply certain equipment?

◄ Are there any extras that he will make available, such as centerpieces, candles, decor items, and other props?

◄ Does he have a staff, or do you need to hire servers and bartenders? Is he able to provide complete bar service?

◄ If he has a staff, are their services included in the per-guest charge? If he doesn't, who does he recommend hiring? It's best to hire one server for every ten guests.

◄ Can he guarantee that you will have his regular staff, and not overload employees, serving your party?

◄ When do you have to let him know the number of guests? How many unexpected guests is he including?

◄ If he uses your facilities and equipment, will your bill be less?

◄ Does their service include cleaning up afterward? If so, is this included in the bill?

◄ At what time will they arrive?

◄ How much are tax and gratuity? Is the gratuity or service charge included in your bill?

◄ Does he work with any florists, photographers, bands, or others with whom you can get a package deal?

◄ Is there a cancellation fee, and if so, how much is it, and what are the conditions regarding it?

Asking these questions before your event helps prevent chaos during it. When planning your meal, consider guests who may not eat certain foods for religious reasons, because they're on a special diet, or because of allergics. It's best to have your menu planned when you invite your guests so you can tell them what you will be serving. This provides them with the opportunity to decline rather than go and not eat, which would be uncomfortable for both of you. You can offer to prepare something else just for them, or chat with the caterer about adjusting the dish in question so your guest who is allergic can eat it also.

Don't lose sight of the fact that although you hired a caterer, this is still your party. While it's best to stay out of the kitchen, you do have every right to tell her how you want other things done. Let her know that you'd like the food presented in attractive, and possibly even unusual ways, if it fits the theme of your event. Often it is simple things that can make an event spectacular. This includes which foods you want prepared if you've already planned your menu; what the servers are to wear (black, white, or colors); how you would like the food to be served (buffet style, on platters, on the table, or to each person individually by the servers); how much alcohol the bartender is allowed to put in the drinks and how she is to handle those who have a few too many. If you want her to use your equipment or dishes, let that be known. Let her know at what time you want the appetizers served and the meal to begin. If your guests will be served their food already on their plates, be sure to specify the size of the portion to be served on each plate. You don't want so much on them that everything is mixed or falls off, but on the other hand, you don't want to serve too little and leave your guests hungry. Having your party done your way may very well cost extra. Be sure to ask your caterer, or you may be in for a big surprise when you get your bill.

Price Quotes

It's essential that you get price quotes in writing. If there is a general category of "extras" included, ask exactly what they are and how much each costs. Some of these little extras have a not-so-little charge attached to them that can add up very quickly. Extras normally include tips, valet parking, service charges for staying longer, taxes, delivery charges, coat checking, and damage liability deposits. At some events you are also legally required to have a law enforcement officer, firefighter, or ambulance personnel on the premises. This, of course, can be an extra cost.

Don't let your caterer convince you to go over your budget. He needs to work appropriately within it, not overextend it. On the other hand, if you change your mind about the menu many times or make other additions, you can't expect your bill to stay the same. Be sure to sign a contract with the caterer that includes the date, time, and location of the event, his duties, cost, and the date the contract was signed.

Including a liability clause that protects guests and the caterer's staff is a good idea, as is weather insurance if the event is to be held outdoors.

Typical Charges

Some caterers charge a flat rate, but most are likely to charge per person based upon the services they provide. Be sure to ask whether gratuities are included in the charge per person. If not, the head server gets 15 to 20 percent of your bill, with the specification that it is to be divided among the staff. When working with only one or two servers or bartenders, each receives 15 to 20 percent of your bill. Each caterer is different, so settle the issue of when to pay a caterer as soon as you plan the menu. More often than not, your caterer will ask for a down payment before the event. This amount is usually 15 to 50 percent of the total bill. Be prepared to pay your caterer the remainder either before the event begins or immediately after it, before she leaves. Note, too, that some caterers charge extra if they have to stay later than the agreed-upon time. Most individuals and corporations aren't extended credit.

Working with Your Caterer

Once your caterer has arrived and gotten situated, leave her to her work. Have faith in her. The only way she can best do her job is if you're out of the way. You know what they say: "Too many cooks spoil the broth."

There are a few things you can do to give your party that extra-special quality. Make sure plates that are supposed to be warm or cold are. Check the appearance of the servers. They should be neatly dressed, well groomed, and professional. Encourage and foster a positive attitude within them if they don't already have one. Remember, your reputation may rest on the service your guests receive. These little details make an ordinary dinner or event extraordinary and memorable. They also make your guests feel special.

Finally, but most importantly, don't forget to thank your caterer for a job well done. If you were so impressed with her services that you're sure you're going to hire her for your next event, telling her is a great idea. It's sure to make her day! Sending a written thank-you note is also an appreciative gesture.

Hotel and Restaurant Catering

If you hold your gathering or conference at a hotel or restaurant, keep in mind that you will usually have to use their catering facilities. They may not be as flexible or do as many services as an independent caterer, so be sure to find out exactly what services you'll receive. Most of the questions that you would ask any caterer apply in this situation, so be sure to include them when asking about their banquet or catering facilities. Also be sure to find out how you'll be billed. Will these services be included in the price for holding the event there, or will you receive a separate bill for them? Are tax and gratuity included in this price? If not, 15 percent of your bill is an appropriate tip. Again, be sure to get all agreements in writing.

There are other practices you need to be aware of when dealing with hotels and conference centers to ensure that your meeting or event is held as planned. One is that if you don't reserve any, or what the hotel considers to be enough, sleeping rooms, or know for sure that no one from your group will be spending the night at the hotel, the hotel may "bump" or cancel your group so that a group that will be occupying sleeping rooms can hold its conference or event there instead. Also, if your group won't be drinking alcohol or frequenting the bar, the hotel or restaurant may replace you on the schedule with a group that will. The hotel or restaurant can implement this cancellation policy usually from 60 to 90 days before your event. This means that even after spending a year planning your event, you may find out two months beforehand that you have no where to hold it. If a more profitable offer comes along, the hotel or restaurant isn't going to turn it down. Ask about this policy in all hotels and restaurants that you're considering as locations for your event. Depending upon the particular establishment, it may be possible to get this cancellation policy waived. Read all confirmation agreements very carefully.

18 Gift Giving

Giving gifts is almost as much fun as receiving them, especially when you've taken great pains to select just the right gift for a person, and he is thrilled with it. Yet, what do you bring to a host you don't know well? What about giving gifts to fellow executives or executives from other companies? What about when you know you need to give a gift, but you don't know what to buy? And what about when you don't even know whether you should give a gift? Whoever thought gift giving could be so complicated?

BUSINESS GIFTS

Giving business gifts can be a little tricky because many companies have policies prohibiting it or limiting gifts to a certain dollar amount so the gifts are not considered bribes. Be sure you know a company's policies before giving anyone in your company or in another firm any type of gift. You don't want to make it look as though you're buying someone off or buttering them up to offer you a good deal. And always be sure to enclose a card that has a personalized message signed by you.

Besides the annual holiday gift, there are several other occasions on which you may give a business gift. Some of these are to congratulate, thank, encourage, apologize, and wish someone good luck. When a gift giving occasion arises, give the present when the event happens, not months later when it won't mean as much. Getting holiday presents in July just doesn't mean the same as getting them in December.

The key to giving business gifts is to make them appropriate. Don't give personal items unless you and the recipient are very good friends. Match your gift to the person's lifestyle, not yours. Don't give him artwork just because you like it; he may not. Asking his secretary or spouse about his interests is a good way to come up with appropriate gift ideas. Be very careful about the types of gifts you give members of the opposite sex. Very personal or very extravagant gifts, such as jewelry, have no place in the office. Neither do presents that are sexually suggestive.

It is not standard practice to give gifts to your boss unless you have worked for her for a very long time or are very close friends. If your boss gives you a gift first, it is okay to reciprocate with a modest, impersonal gift. Unless senior-level management members plan to attend all employees' weddings, they should decline the invitations to all but those on their immediate staff. There is no need for such an executive to send a present when declining to attend. And it is not standard for employees to give their supervisors a wedding present. Business associates usually give wedding presents that reflect the value or strength of the relationship and that are based upon what they can afford.

COST GUIDELINES

Deciding how much to spend on a gift and selecting a particular gift often go hand in hand. Unless your company has a fund especially for gifts, you're probably going to have to pay out of pocket for any gifts you give. If someone in the office is taking up a collection to buy a gift for John's birthday or Sally's new baby, you don't have to feel obligated to contribute. If these collections are becoming expensive or if you just don't want to contribute for whatever reason, politely decline. You are not required to give an excuse when you decline.

Some suggested amounts to spend on gifts for clients are as follows: if you are a junior executive or mid-manager, $10 to $25; for upper managers, $25 to $50; and for senior managers, $50 to $100 on gifts for close business friends and preferred customers. Spending more than $100 on a gift happens only once in a great while and not for just for any occasion. If an employee is giving a gift to a supervisor, the acceptable price is around $25. It is standard for bosses to spend about the same amount on gifts for their secretaries, yet they can spend more based upon how long he has worked for him, and the nature of their friendship. The amount to spend on gifts for a fellow executive in your company is based upon your relationship with him.

GIFT IDEAS

Flowers and Plants

What you give as a gift obviously depends upon the occasion. Flowers and plants are appropriate for almost any occasion. Still, some people like one or the other better, so consider their preference. Plants and flowers also very easy to send because you can order them over the phone, have the florist deliver them, and send them almost anywhere. Flowers and plants as a business gift should be sent to the office. Plants and flowers sent as a thank you for a dinner or party are sent to the home. It is best to send a plant that requires little attention to someone in the hospital, but once she is at home, it's okay to send flowers.

Collectibles

One trend in business gift giving today is collectibles. Collectibles provide you with a wide range of gift ideas, and something that you can add to for the next gift giving occasion. This makes your thinking of gifts for the future much easier. Appropriate collectibles range from handblown glass paperweights, porcelain, and baseball cards, to pen sets and cards of all kinds. Again, consider your relationship with the person and their interests in making a choice of collectibles.

Tickets

Tickets are another gift that is much appreciated. You could give a set of tickets to a special concert or sports event. You might even attach the tickets to flowers or a plant and have them delivered. In fact, flowers delivered with a pair of tickets is the most popular business gift today.

Wine

Wine is appropriate not only as a gift for a dinner host, but also as a business gift. Again, you need to use some discretion when giving wine. Be sure the person to whom you are giving it enjoys and appreciates good wine. When giving wine, after-dinner liqueurs, and good brandy, you don't need to be so specific. These are all beverages that, when given as gifts, are meant to be shared with others. Thus, they are likely to be consumed at a future gathering and are less likely to occupy space in a person's cupboard, even if he doesn't usually drink the variety you've given him.

Food

Food is another great gift. And half the fun of getting such a gift is sharing it with others. Almost any type of food is acceptable. Nuts, cheeses, jams and jellies, candy, homemade breads, cakes and cookies, and fresh fruit are some more common items. You might even want to give a cookbook with the specialty food item. If you want to give something a little more special, try caviar, fresh lobsters, or frozen steaks flown in, imported foods, and special ice creams and sauces. Your choices are unlimited. Gourmet shops and mail-order catalogs offer a wide selection of unique food items that enables you to pick the food that is just right for the occasion. Because it's packaged and shipped properly, you also don't have to worry about the recipient opening the box to find a gift of moldy cheese or rotten fruit. Giving foods that are grown or manufactured in your area, such as smoked salmon from Seattle, wild rice from California or Minnesota, country hams from Missouri, pecan pie from Georgia, cheese from Wisconsin, and lobsters from Massachusetts personalize your gift even more.

Accessories

Accessories are a terrific gift if you know the person's interests. Glasses, serving trays, and coasters are just a few ideas. Avoid bed-and-bath items for business gifts.

BIRTHDAY GIFTS

Don't be disappointed if you're not showered with gifts from business associates on your birthday. Birthday gifts in the business world are almost nonexistent. Cards or a get-together with close friends are usually the only gifts given, and even this occurs only on special birthdays, such as your fortieth.

NEW BABY

Congratulate an associate with whom you work closely on the arrival of his new baby with flowers, a card, or handwritten note of congratulations, or a small gift for the baby such as a rattle, baby mug, or spoon. It's proper to send a gift when an important client, customer, or company director has a baby also. These gifts are often silver and engraved and carry the company's logo. Some ideas include baby mugs and spoons, picture frames, and rattles.

RETIREMENT GIFTS

A retirement gift is one you will want to spend some time selecting. Choose a fine gift that honors the many years of service and dedication the employee has given the company. Don't feel that you have to go into debt or buy lavish plaques or gold and diamonds as a gift, though. Sometimes a more personal item such as a high-quality, gold-embossed leather scrapbook of the person's accomplishments shown through newspaper articles, photographs, and other publicity is appreciated more. It has also become quite traditional to compile a notebook of letters from people who have worked with the person over the years. All of these gifts are something that will be cherished and passed down through the generations.

Everyone could pitch in to send the retiree and her spouse on that trip they've always wanted to take. You could have a framed portrait done. You also could give her items related to how she will be spending her retirement, such as golfing or traveling. Any gift that is elegant and that the retiree will enjoy will be appreciated.

GIFTS FOR THE HOST

Usually when you're invited to a person's home for a meal or party, you should bring a small gift for the host. Acceptable gifts for the host are flowers, wine, or candy. Use your common sense here. Flowers may not be so beautiful if your host has allergies. If you know it is acceptable to bring flowers, either a single special flower or a good-sized bouquet is fine. But don't overdo by making it too big.

Don't give wine or liquor to someone who doesn't drink, is underage, or is a recovering alcoholic. And when giving liquor, it's best to know what your host drinks. Don't give gin if she prefers Scotch. As stated in the wine section, when giving wine, you don't need to be so specific. Even if your host doesn't typically drink the type of wine you've brought, it's not likely to sit on a shelf collecting dust.

Chocolates and other candies are a great gift, but don't tempt a dieter or a diabetic.

If you do bring wine, don't expect your host to serve it with the meal. He may have already selected the wine for the meal. Bringing desserts or other food items isn't recommended, because it only makes your host feel obligated to serve them right away. He has the meal planned, and your surprise additions weren't included on the menu. If you do bring wine or desserts, indicate to the host that you don't expect him to serve them with the meal by saying something such as, "I brought this for you to enjoy privately, later."

There are many other small items that make great gifts for a host. If you know she needs a particular accessory, she'd probably appreciate that a lot more than another box of candy. Unusual or small food items, such as spices and cooking wines, and small kitchen utensils that you have found especially helpful are good for ideas for the host who likes to cook. Again, match your gift to your host's interests. If you're not sure, flowers, wine, or candy are usually safest.

Present your gift to your host when you arrive. It doesn't have to be wrapped, but it may be if you'd like. Including a card is not necessary and is not usually included, since you will be giving your gift directly to your host.

RECEIVING GIFTS

If you receive a business gift that is too expensive, let the person know that, for policy reasons, you are unable to accept the gift. You can send the person a note letting them know you appreciate their thoughtfulness, but company policy will not allow you to keep the gift. Return the gift as gracefully as you can right away.

When opening a gift you do not care for, say, "Oh how nice, thank you" as positively as you can. Let it go at that.

PRESENTATION

How your gift is wrapped and presented is as important as the gift itself. Artfulness is the key. Wrapping paper embellished with metallics, faux marble finishes, paisley designs, silk moire, rice paper, and shiny tissue papers all make a package look very special.

Covered boxes and gift bags can simplify things for those who are clumsy at gift wrapping. Also, they can be used by the recipient to store other items later. However you choose to wrap your gifts, be sure they represent the feeling you want to give. Don't commit a major faux pas by forgetting to remove the price tags, and remember—gift giving is a year-round experience.

19 Persons with Disabilities

People are often unsure of how to act around a person with a disability. However, with few exceptions, in matters of etiquette persons with disabilities should not be treated any differently than an able-bodied person. Most of the rules of etiquette are really no more than a matter of common sense and having consideration for that person. Whenever you talk with a disabled person, always speak directly to them, not to their companion.

HANDS OFF

Some people are sensitive when others touch and move around their very valuable and personal possessions. Why should a person with a disability be any different? The possessions we're referring to are the person's wheelchair, cane, crutches, or any other devices that provide mobility assistance. These items should never be moved away from the person. Crutches, wheelchairs, etc. are considered part of the person. If you wouldn't touch their arm then you also don't touch their mobility aids. If one of these items must be moved, be sure to first ask the person's permission explaining that it is blocking an area, and let them know where the item will be located. Likewise, don't distract or pet service dogs even if they're cute and appear to not be working.

TO THE RESCUE?

The first thing to remember when you see a person with a disability, whether he is on crutches, using a cane, or in a wheelchair, is that he still may be very capable of doing many things for himself. Don't automatically assume that the person needs assistance. Always ask the person whether or not he needs or even wants help, whether it's carrying packages, going up stairs, crossing a street, or whatever. Offering to help someone is never wrong, but don't help them if they don't need it. Just remember it's up to that person to accept your offer. Only when the person is in extreme physical danger is it okay to assist a person in some other way without asking, but even then, help carefully. You don't want to put them in more danger by catching them off guard or by doing something without their knowledge.

If the person accepts your offer of assistance, be sure to listen to what she wants done and how it should be done. Disabled people know what is best for them and the best ways to do it. Never disregard their instructions. After hearing the person's instructions, determine whether or not you can do what they want done. You may not be physically or otherwise capable of doing it well. You can make a situation worse by only partially completing their request or by doing a poor job.

HOLD THAT DOOR!

Doors and elevators are sometimes difficult enough for able-bodied people to use. It's common courtesy to open a door for a person with a disability, just as it is for an able-bodied person. There are a few rules to follow, though, to make it go smoothly. First, have the door open as the person is approaching it. Waiting until she is already in the doorway and possibly leaning on the doorknob for support is too late. Let the person go through the doorway unassisted if she's able. Trying to fit the two of you through at one time or grabbing the person's arm, crutches, cane, or wheelchair isn't going to work.

The procedure for holding an elevator door is basically the same as for holding a regular door. Make sure the person is completely inside before allowing the door to close, and if you're not riding the elevator, ask the person if he can reach the buttons. If not, press the button for the appropriate floor before you leave the person in the elevator or make sure someone in the elevator will do it for him. When you are on the elevator with someone trying to get out, step up and hold the door open button for them to get out.

DON'T GET PUSHY

If you're hesitant about pushing someone in a wheelchair, don't worry—they may be just as hesitant about having you push them. Just take it slowly and listen to their instructions. Most people in motorized wheelchairs don't need to be pushed unless their wheelchairs are broken or external conditions make it difficult to use them. Some of these conditions are slick surfaces, steep ramps, thick carpeting, a bumpy street, or tricky situations such as crowded rooms and tight corners.

People in manual wheelchairs may need to be pushed more often. Always ask the person whether or not she would like to be pushed, and ask where she'd like to go. Push slowly and carefully, watching out for objects on the floor, rough or soft spots, and anything else that may upset the stability of the chair.

ONE STEP AT A TIME

Stairs, steps, and curbs might not seem like much of a challenge to an able-bodied person, but to someone with a disability, stairs, steps, and curbs can be as tough to climb as mountains. Be careful when you assist someone up or down stairs, as they are a common place for disasters to occur. Before you help someone in a wheelchair maneuver stairs or a curb, ask to make sure they really do need your help. Going up steps requires that you lean the chair back so the front wheels are raised off the floor, and then pull the chair up the stairs with the chair facing backwards. To go down, push the person frontwards. Ask what the person prefers. Again, raise the chair so the front wheels are off the floor and the person is resting back into the chair, not leaning forward as if he is about to fall out, and keep the wheels up until the chair is entirely down the steps.

To help someone who is able to walk but not well, extend your arm for support and balance as you walk alongside. Grabbing the person by the arm isn't as helpful as you might think. When assisting someone who is able to walk up and down stairs, precede them down and follow them up. This will put you in the best position to stabilize them if they should fall. Breaking a persons fall is okay, but trying to catch someone is dangerous for both people. Oftentimes, people who know they are prone to falling can handle things more safely by themselves.

FALLS

The best way to help a person with a disability avoid falls is to leave enough room for others to move around them. If he should fall, ask if he needs your help. It's quite possible that he won't. Many mobility-impaired people are skilled at and better off getting up on their own. Well-meaning others often only get in the way when they try to help.

ARCHITECTURAL BARRIERS

The three most common architectural barriers that cause difficulty for individuals with a disability are parking places, stairs, and rest rooms. If you are planning on taking a person with a disability anywhere, whether to a restaurant, mall, government office, house, or office building, check to see whether it is accessible for her first. Call ahead and discuss it with the person. If it's not and you have to encounter these barriers together, don't force help on the person in getting over them. And before you do help, make sure you can handle it physically.

Handicapped parking places need to be larger than those for everyone else to accommodate larger vehicles and wheelchairs. These places should be close to the main or handicap entrance of the building. Be ready to help with stairs if necessary. If possible, avoid going places that have any stairs and no elevators if you know neither of you will be able to climb them. Rest rooms should be large enough to allow the person to easily move a wheelchair around in them. The door has to be wide enough to get the chair through it first. Having a handicapped stall equipped with a hand rail is another necessity. Be sure to check State and Federal codes including the Americans with Disabilities Act (ADA).

ASK THEM OUT

If you invite a person with a disability to attend a function, it's often necessary and at the very least, considerate, to let them know well in advance about the event so he can fit it into his schedule, arrange for transportation and make any other preparations. But don't make the mistake of thinking that a person with a disability doesn't like to or can't do anything on the spur of the moment. The only way to find out if they'd like to join you is to ask.

Meet at a place that you have checked out beforehand and have okayed with the person so you both know it'll be accessible for her, or meet at a place she recommends. She knows better than anyone else which places are most accessible for her. It's acceptable to offer to meet at your house, but it may be easier to meet at hers instead.

When considering transportation, you may offer to pick the person up, but if you do, make sure your vehicle can accommodate any special needs such as a wheelchair. Offer to help the person into your car, and assist according to his instructions. Remember, too, that many people with a disability do drive, and it may be easier for them to drive their own vehicle than to have you pick them up.

When selecting a restaurant, choose one that has ample space between tables and chairs. Arrange for a table close to the entry and on the same level if possible. Be sure to tell the person, "Let me know if I can help you in any way." They will then ask if they need help. Generally volunteer in this way only once, and then don't keep asking or helping when not asked.

ASK THEM OVER

When you invite a person with a disability to your home, consider doing the following: Ask if they have any special needs. Inform the person of any barriers in your home, such as stairs and rest rooms. Arrange for the person to let you know when he will arrive. You can do this by having him honk a horn, call when leaving home, or do any other thing that both of you agree upon. This allows you to offer any help that may be needed to get the person into the house and ensures that he won't be sitting outside the door waiting.

If this person is in a wheelchair, remove some of the clutter and furniture from the room. Try to provide a place that is sociable but out of the way of traffic for the person to sit. As with any guest, be sure to introduce her and make sure she's not left out of conversations and sitting alone. If the person has a cane or crutches, she can place them near her.

Be aware of what your guest can and can't eat, and plan accordingly. Take into consideration, too, the type of impairment your guest has. If he can't use his arms and hands well, don't make finger foods or foods that are difficult to cut or eat unless you will help.

Seat her at the table in a position that is most comfortable for her. At the table, remove one of the chairs before she comes into the room so she has a spot at the table, like everyone else. This may be at the head or the side of the table or even slightly away from it. Offer to feed your guest, if necessary. Alternate serving her and eating your meal. Ask her what she would like to eat next. Be willing to serve her meal on a large, low, or high table or on a tray— whatever is easiest for them.

WHEN YOU VISIT

You may find that you go to the person's house more than he will come to yours just because it's easier for him. Be a gracious guest. Be willing to serve yourself; don't expect to be catered to if it's easier for you to get your own beverage from the refrigerator. Help your host with whatever may need to be done, but don't pester him to accept your help if he declines your offer. It's his house. Clean up before you leave, but don't put cups, plates, or anything else in places where your friend will have trouble reaching them after you've left. If you've moved any furniture, move it back to where you found it.

FACE–TO–FACE CONVERSATION

Don't give a person in a wheelchair a stiff neck by making her look up to talk to you. It's best to sit facing her at eye level, but depending on the situation, you may have to stand. Do whatever is easiest and most comfortable for both of you.

CONVERSATION TOPICS

When it comes to choosing conversation topics, let your relationship be your guide. The same rules that apply to any friendship or relationship apply to your conversation with a person who has a disability. Use your best judgment on subjects that are of a personal or private nature.

CUSTOMERS WITH DISABILITIES

Whether you work as a salesperson, cashier, server, health care professional, or in any other career in which you serve people with disabilities, there are a few considerations to keep in mind to be more helpful to the customer. First, you need to be able to give this customer some basic information that will be very important to her. This includes knowing where the elevators, rest rooms, and stairs with hand rails are, knowing whether or not there is handicapped parking, making sure dressing rooms are large enough for a wheelchair, and being able to describe any types of architectural barriers. To be most accommodating, you need to be able to accurately give all of this information over the phone. This lets the person know what to expect before she gets there and allows her to make any necessary arrangements.

Keep the floors clean and dry everywhere you work. Dirt, grease, water, clutter, and other stray items on the floor are very dangerous to someone who's in a wheelchair or who has difficulty walking. When there's grease and dirt on the floor, such as in a service station, don't expect a person in a wheelchair to go through it, because the dirt will get on her wheels and then on her hands.

Assist the person with items out of her reach. This includes both high and low shelves. Offer to carry her shopping basket or bags if necessary. People in wheelchairs, cannot always carry these items.

As a cashier or teller, you can make transactions easier for the disabled person by serving him at a lower counter or desk or even offering to let him sit if standing or walking is difficult. To those in a wheelchair, offer a hard surface, such as a hardcover book or clipboard, to use as a writing surface. Be prepared to write the person's check, too, but remember to let him sign it. It may also be necessary for you to assist with money and coupons and help him get merchandise on the counter. Package merchandise as requested. In some cases, paper bags may be easier to handle than plastic, and vice versa. Bags with handles may be needed. Never assume that a person needs you to do all of this for him, though. Always ask before taking any action, and be patient.

Here are a few tips to remember if you work in a restaurant. Seat a person in a wheelchair in a spacious location near the entryway, if possible. Make sure there is enough room between the table and chairs and between other tables and chairs. If the person will remain in the same chair during the meal, remove the regular chair before the person gets to the table. Don't move the person's wheelchair out of their reach. This is a safety and respect issue for the person who uses the wheelchair. However, as mentioned earlier, if a person's wheelchair must be moved, don't forget to ask first. If the person has crutches, seat him near a wall so he can lean his crutches or cane against it. You may need to help transfer the person from his wheelchair to the regular chair, move salt and pepper shakers, glasses, and so on closer to him if he has difficulty using his arms. He may also request that his food, such as meat or vegetables, be cut into bite-sized pieces in the kitchen before being served. It is appropriate to offer this service and also to check on this person a little more often than you do others just to see if there's anything else he may need.

As a professional, you must design your office in compliance with the state and federal—Americans with Disabilities Act (ADA) accessibility codes. You might want to begin by calling your state council on disability to help you find the information you need. State codes are often stricter than federal codes. This usually means having as few architectural barriers as possible and letting the person know about any she will encounter. Have one or two sturdy, medium-height chairs with arms for those who find it difficult to sit in or rise from a chair. Have your bell or buzzer in a location convenient for a person in a wheelchair so you'll know when she arrives. Let your staff know that this person will be coming so they will be able to assist her in whatever ways are necessary. Remember that this person may not move as quickly as an able-bodied person and may need a longer appointment because of it. Eliminate the need for the person to have to move around unnecessarily. Bring paperwork to her. Keep the scheduled appointment time as the person may have had to make special transportation arrangements.

PARKING

You will want to ask the person about parking before he comes to meet with you. Find out if he has difficulty walking or how far he can walk. If you ask him a few questions, you will probably be able to suggest a parking place that fits his needs. Most building parking lots, even if they are designated "contract only" lots will sometimes be able to accommodate the special needs of a disabled person. A great suggestion comes from an attorney who calls the supervisor of the contract lot for her office building to see if an exception can be made for her disabled client to park close to the office. So far, every time she has needed to have a person with a disability park close to her office, the parking attendant has been accommodating.

20 Sports Etiquette

Etiquette for both players and spectators during games is important. I'll begin with some general pointers that apply to many sports. If you need to borrow equipment, wait for another player to volunteer the use of golf clubs, racquet, and so on. It's often hard to withhold help and advice, but don't give unsolicited suggestions about how to improve an individual's play until it is requested. When a person is in the middle of play or a performance, don't distract him in any way. Stay at a reasonable distance, silent and motionless, whenever a player or athlete needs maximum concentration.

GOLF

It is the obligation of every player to learn certain practices and customs that help to make the game pleasurable for all players. Actually if you are a beginning golfer, you should place a higher priority on learning etiquette than on learning anything else about the game. Many experts have said that if you know golfing etiquette and can make a good first swing (the only time anyone ever looks at you the whole game), you've got it made. This may not be entirely true, but knowing golfing etiquette will help your confidence.

Taking care of the golf course is one of the most important parts of golf etiquette. In the game of golf, if a lump of turf is dislodged by a player's club when making a swing, it is called a *divot*. Whenever you make a divot in the fairway, you must replace it.

If your shot to the green is high, the ball may "dent" the green. A special, small, two-pronged tool is available to help you repair these ball marks and fluff up the turf. As one avid golfer remarked, true golf etiquette regarding green repair is to repair "yours and one other." It is essential to keep all golf clubs and carts off the greens. Whenever you play out of a trap or bunker (frequently referred to as a sand trap), be sure to rake and smooth these as well.

Distracting other players is one of the biggest social errors of the golf game. Do not talk or yell to another player or make any other disruptive noise. Be still and quiet when your fellow golfer is hitting. Never move into another players line of vision or walk through her putting line. Stay out of her line of sight. And never allow your shadow to cross a ball or to fall in the line of another person's putt. Don't stand too close to anyone hitting a ball.

For those people organizing golf events for business, play "best ball" at each hole. It is an excellent social event, it is low stress, and it builds team spirit. Asking total strangers to play stroke golf or match golf is too stressful and not as much fun.

When you start to play, it is your responsibility to be on time. Failure to be on time will result in forfeiture of your starting time. Most golf courses are very strict about starting on time because they are booked full. Begin playing on the hole the starter advises for your group. Usually it is hole number 1 or hole number 10.

Time is particularly important in golf. Any avid golfer will tell you, "Slow play kills the game." If you can't keep up, walk your ball to be sure you keep up with your group. Definitely pick up your ball after making ten strokes on a hole. Be conscious of time, and walk quickly between plays. Play in turn and be ready to hit when it is your turn. Taking a stance and grounding the golf club before taking a swing is called *addressing the ball*. Grounding your club in a bunker is not permitted. Do not address the ball too long, and take no more than one practice swing. Do not hit extra balls on the course. Walk off the golf green to record your scores. Allow groups that are playing faster than yours to "play through" your group. Place your clubs on the ground between the green and the next tee.

As with most social and business occasions, wearing the proper attire on the golf course communicates a great deal about the individual. Most clubs do have dress codes. If you are to be a guest at a club you haven't visited previously, you should inquire of your host or the club as to their dress code. Generally shorts are permitted so long as they are at least mid-thigh length. Men are often required to wear colored shirts and women are discouraged from wearing halter tops.

As with every other sport, there are safety factors to consider. First, never take a chance of hitting another player. If there is ever any doubt that you might hit someone, be sure to wait to hit before you swing. If one of your balls should take off in another player's direction, always yell "Fore!" "Fore!" is the warning cry to any person in the way of play. If you ever hear anyone yelling "Fore," be sure to take cover. It is not acceptable to hit a ball into the foursome in front of you to remind them they are playing slowly.

Never throw clubs, curse, or make a big show of anger. Golf, like all sports, is supposed to be fun. Remind yourself, "A bad day of golf is still better than a good day at work."

Besides learning golf etiquette, you may want to refer to a book on golf to learn the other fundamentals, rules, and frequently used terms. The most important thing in any situation is to do what you need beforehand to feel comfortable. Keep your advice to yourself. Treat your fellow players the way you would like to be treated. Congratulate a player on a good shot and pretend you didn't see a bad one.

TENNIS

As with golf, manners both on and off the tennis court are an important part of the game. These manners and customs are not included in the official rules, but throughout the years they have become accepted as part of the game.

Before the Game

As with all sports, learn the more important rules of tennis. Find a good book at the library or in the bookstore. Or, ask a friend who has experience playing tennis to teach you the more important rules of the game. You may want to watch a game or two on TV.

Before beginning a friendly game, make sure your opponent or your group agrees on how rules will be enforced. Also agree on the length of the warmup. Ask your opponent or partner if she'd like to practice warmup strokes with you. Toss a coin to decide the choice of serve and side of court.

Dress code is very important when playing tennis, so always make sure you look your best. Aim for a balance between comfortable, practical, and traditional tennis apparel. If you walk onto the court wearing scruffy or unsuitable clothing, you could give your opponent a psychological advantage. Wear neat and clean clothing and tennis shoes. You might consider calling the tennis club you will be playing at to check their guidelines. If you are playing in a tournament, you may be required to wear a T-shirt or blouse, shorts or skirt, and tennis shoes.

Playing the Game

Being courteous to other players is part of being a good tennis player. When playing, always keep your voice down so as not to distract the other players. If your ball rolls onto someone else's court, do not run after it until their point is over. Return a ball from someone else's court only when you finish the point with your opponent. Never lean on or touch the net, even after you have stopped playing.

It's great to give your doubles partner encouragement during the game with phrases such as "nice return." However, don't have a long conversation with your partner, as it could delay the game. Even in a friendly tennis match, concentrate on the game.

It's frustrating when you think an official may have made a wrong call against you or your partner, but good manners dictate that you obey the decisions of all officials. If you have a question about the call, ask it after the game.

Officiating your own match is tricky, but if you practice good manners, you'll be on your way to following the rules. For instance, you must call all line plays on your side of the net, and your opponent must call all line plays on hers. If you see a ball go outside the line on your opponent's side, good manners and the rules dictate that you call an "out" against yourself. Likewise, if you don't see your opponent's ball go out on your side of the net, you must call that "in" and score a point for your opponent.

Don't serve until your opponent is ready, and always call out the score before each serve. If the receiver wasn't ready, call a "let" serve. You'll then play the point over. Also call a "let" if a ball from another court interferes with your game. If you know that a serve is out, do not return it.

If you make a foot fault when serving, call it. It is unfair to take advantage of the other player just because she can't see your error. Make a call against yourself if you touch or reach over the net or make other errors your opponent doesn't notice. At the end of the match, always shake hands with your opponent.

Being a Polite Spectator

Being a polite tennis spectator usually means being a quiet one. Wait until after a point is played to ask out loud for a score or to applaud a great play. Don't make distracting movements or move from seat to seat while play is in progress. Try not to walk across or behind a court until the game is over.

When watching a game, accept the decisions of game officials as final. Show the players you appreciated their efforts by applauding after a match.

RACQUETBALL

To make racquetball fun and safe, good court etiquette is especially important. Two tips before covering the written and unwritten rules of the game: Most athletic clubs do not allow black-soled shoes to be worn because they leave hard-to-remove black marks on the court. Also, for your safety, eye guards are strongly recommended. Eye guards are an inexpensive investment and protect your eyes from injury by either a racquet or a ball.

Playing the Game

Providing your playing partner with an unobstructed view and path to the ball is the first rule of racquetball etiquette. Every player is entitled to a fair chance to see and return the ball. So, when you hit the ball, move in a direction that gives your playing opponent an unobstructed approach and enough room to take a full swing. Of course, this is not always possible in the fast-paced game of racquetball. If your opponent feels he was sufficiently hindered in his game, he can call *hinder*, which means the point is played over. Often the easiest way to get out of your opponent's way is to hit the ball and then take a circular route. This provides your playing partner ample room, yet keeps you properly positioned on the court.

If it is obvious that your opponent is about to hit the ball down along the side wall, you must not move into the lane along the side wall to block the flight of the ball to the front wall. This is called an *avoidable hinder*, which occurs when a player deliberately obstructs an opponent's play. The offending player automatically loses the rally when an avoidable hinder is called. You don't hear much about avoidable hinders when playing socially; people who use these tactics aren't often asked to play.

A primary complaint of racquetball players is opponents who don't stay out of the way of the ball so they can play their game. Whether intent to crowd, clumsiness, loss of balance, or poor stroke has put you in the way of the ball, get out of the way so the other player can play. Each player needs to allow the other player access to the ball, allowing everyone to play the game without interference.

Each player deserves a fair chance to hit the ball when it is her turn. Obviously, then, you may not distract, scream, or stamp your feet when your opponent is preparing to return the ball.

Fair Play

Honesty, courtesy, respect for your opponent, and a sense of fair play are unwritten rules of court etiquette. Treat your opponent the way you would like to be treated. When you're not playing in a tournament, give your opponent enough room to hit the ball to any part of the front wall. If you treat your opponent this way, she will probably reciprocate.

If you hit your opponent with a ball, apologize immediately, and allow them to recover—getting hit can hurt—then play the point over. This usually happens either because you lost control of the shot or because your opponent was slow to move out of the way. Getting hit with the ball is all part of the game of racquetball.

If you are unsure of a call, if you don't know whether your ball skipped or whether you hit the ball before it bounced twice on the floor—offer to replay the point. Still, don't stop play if you are unsure about the call. Continue playing a point, then ponder the situation after the rally is completed. Reviewing both written and unwritten rules of the game with your opponent before starting the game often works well. Decide with your playing opponent before starting to play whether to play out all questionable calls or to rely on the receiving player to make calls.

It is acceptable during play to take a few seconds to catch your breath, even if the other player is ready. But don't stall. If you need more than just a breather, call a time-out. In tournament competition, the ball must be served within ten seconds after the referee calls out the score. In an official game, short time-outs are limited in number. In a social game, you can rest whenever both players want to.

Lap Swimming

Most athletic clubs ask swimmers to shower before using the swimming pool. They also ask swimmers to shower again before going back into the pool after using the rest room, sauna, or steam room. If you are suffering from a cold or another communicable illness, or if you have open sores, cuts, or blisters, you are asked to refrain from using the pool.

In most swimming pools where adult lap swim times are posted, the lanes are marked for speed of swimming. Whether the lanes are marked or unmarked, choose your lane carefully based on your speed in relation to other swimmers swimming at the time. The fast lanes are for fast swimmers. Swimming strokes, such as the elementary backstroke and the side stroke are not fast strokes.

If other swimmers are passing you, be considerate and move to the medium or slow lanes. The slow lane is meant for swimmers who wish to swim at a slow pace or who need a safer, more controlled lane.

Swimmers are expected to share swimming lanes fairly and considerately. Check to see if kickboards and pull buoys may be used. Usually they are allowed in lap swimming.

All lap swimming is to be done in a circular pattern. Swim down on the right side of the lane, and back on the right in a straight line. Also, if a fellow swimmer passes you, stay to the right. The easiest way to facilitate passing is to stop at the end of the lane and let the faster swimmer go on. Avoid excessive splashing. If you feel faint, dizzy, or out of breath while swimming, stop and rest.

When you have completed your lap swimming, leave the pool or move to a non-lap swim area, so your fellow swimmers will have room to make turns.

ATHLETIC CLUBS

After using any exercise equipment such as the stationary bicycles or other exercise equipment, be sure to reset the equipment at its starting position. Since you will usually perspire during a good workout, be sure to wipe down the equipment so it is ready for the next person to use.

When you're in the locker room, store your workout bags and equipment in your locker, on top of the locker, or under the bench. Don't leave your belongings spread out all over the benches and in the aisle.

For the cleanliness and health of others, shaving in the whirlpools, sauna, and steam rooms is usually prohibited. Most clubs also will ask you to shower before entering or reentering whirlpools. And, persons with open or infectious sores are not permitted in whirlpools.

For your own safety, watch the amount of time you spend in whirlpools, saunas, and steam rooms. Do not exceed thirty minutes in the sauna, because excessive exposure can be harmful to your health. For the same reasons, it is a good idea to watch how long you stay in whirlpools and steam rooms. If you are in poor health, consult your physician before using the whirlpool, sauna, or steam room. If you bring your children, keep them out of the whirlpools or check the water temperature. The high temperature of the water can be harmful.

Most athletic clubs try hard to keep their facilities and equipment in top working condition. If you know that a piece of equipment is broken down or that an area of the club needs staff attention, let them know. Most club managers appreciate members helping them out in this way.

A thoughtful gesture is to write positive notes to the manager about any staff person who does an especially good job. These notes are usually read at weekly staff meetings, and the staff person is also notified. Letting staff members know of a job well done keeps them enthusiastic, and therefore friendly and helpful. Their attitude adds to the pleasure of working out at your club. Here's to your health!

PRIVATE BOXES

It's a fun and special experience to have the opportunity to watch an event from a private box. A private box is an enclosure exclusive from the regular seats that is used primarily for entertaining, often for business. When you receive an invitation to a private box, find out what the proper attire is. Men usually wear a sport coat and dress shirt, but attire can range from black tie to casual. Women dress as they would when accompanying a man dressed in this way. The attire to be worn depends on who is entertaining.

Hors d'oeuvres are usually provided at no charge. If you desire additional food, you may purchase it at your own expense.

SPECTATOR BEHAVIOR

The main duty of a spectator is to enjoy herself without interfering with the play or performance or other spectators. For example, standing on the sidelines and blocking the view of those in the front row is not acceptable spectator behavior. Refrain from blocking the view of people behind you by leaping to your feet to get a better view. Otherwise, you'll deserve to hear: "Down in front!"

Offer advice to the sports participant only when you are asked to do so. Don't distract a player in the middle of a point, play, or performance. This means staying quiet and still and a reasonable distance from the participants.

Showing your enthusiasm for your team is certainly appropriate and even expected at sporting events, but do not criticize the other team with loud boos or yelling. Especially in a business entertainment setting where the opposing team may have a fan in your group, it is wise to heed the axiom to "root for yourself, not against your opponent." If you attend with someone who is rooting for the losing team, it is polite to comment on how well that team played and to offer consolation for their defeat.

Cheers, boos, whistles, and catcalls are all a standard part of spectator participation and part of the fun at some events. But one etiquette rule regarding applause applies to all spectators: Applauding a poor shot or a miss, no matter how delighted a spectator may be at the failure, is poor sportsmanship.

As a general rule, applaud at the end of a play or turn, not during it. Keep in mind the sport you are attending. Sometimes cheering and applause are part of the atmosphere, as for boxing or horse racing.

If you must leave your seat during an event, return only when there is a break in the action. Wait at the top of the stairs until time-out or intermission. Return to your seat only when you will not disturb other spectators.

21 Travel Etiquette

AIR TRAVEL

Business travelers seem to have two main complaints. The first is travelers who carry too much luggage onto the plane and crowd everyone around them. The second is seatmates who talk too much. Following are suggestions for how to deal with these two situations.

Carry-on Luggage

Most airlines allow two pieces of carry-on luggage. Businesspeople often travel with one garment bag and another piece of luggage, such as a large briefcase or a small suitcase, that will fit in the top bin above the seat or under the seat in front of them. To fit in the cabin closet, the garment bag should be no larger than 4 inches deep, 23 inches wide, and 45 inches long. For 737 aircraft and larger, the size of the luggage that typically fits under the seat in front of you is 9 inches deep, 14 inches wide, and 22 inches long. To fit in the overhead compartment, the suitcase dimensions should be no more than 14 inches deep, 21 inches wide, and 36 inches long. Because there are many types of aircraft today, you may want to check with your travel agent or the airline to see what type of plane you will be flying in and the dimensions of top bins and underseat space. Be considerate and take up no more than your own space.

Sociability

If you don't feel like talking but your seatmate does, you can simply apologize that you cannot take the time right then to get to know him better and tell him, very politely, that you have much work to do or really need to get some shut-eye. Keep your eyes down and concentrate on your work, or simply give vague, short answers to his inquiries and hope that he will get the point. If worst comes to worst, offer to lend him a newspaper, book, or anything else it takes to keep him occupied. If the person is talking to ease nervousness or fear of flying, set aside that report or keep your eyes open a little longer to listen and reassure him.

Similarly, start a conversation with your seatmate only if she seems interested in talking. You can test whether your seatmate wants to talk with a general question such as "Are you traveling for business or pleasure?" If you get a one-word answer, you should take the hint and not to pursue a conversation.

Reclining Your Seat

Always remember to look behind your seat before reclining so you don't hit someone's knees or head, if they're bending over to put something under their seat. Usually during mealtimes, passengers put their seats back in the upright position. So again, as a precaution, look behind your seat after eating so you don't recline your seat into the passenger behind you who may still be eating.

In-Flight Meals

If you're served a meal on your flight, tear yourself away from your work and be sociable enough to chat with your seatmate. If she doesn't make an effort to talk, don't press the issue. You don't have to get into a lengthy conversation, but a little small talk between seatmates can make a long flight seem shorter and ease tension between you. When eating on a plane, remember your basic table manners and do the best you can with the plasticware and you'll be fine (unless, of course, the plane hits unexpected turbulence!). Placing your napkin in your shirt as a bib is acceptable on a plane, whereas it usually is not at a table. Because your internal organs expand when you're in flight, it's best to limit your food intake. Overeating might cause you to be more uncomfortable than you already are.

Alcoholic Beverages

On economy flights, you'll have to pay for your beer and mixed drinks, but soft drinks are usually free. If you know you're going to want three beers, order and pay for them all at once and with the correct change. It's a good idea, however, to limit your consumption of alcoholic beverages while in the air to no more than one. Flying not only dehydrates the body, but it also causes alcohol to have four times the effect on your body as it would on the ground. Your best bet is to have a glass of plain water or soda water and forego the spirits.

The Flight Attendant

The job of the flight attendants is to ensure your safety and comfort, not to be your personal maid, so don't treat them as such. Forcing the attendant to make many trips and to search for change is a waste of his precious time. Flight attendants are not tipped, but they would greatly appreciate a "thank you" or other expression of your appreciation. Remember to recognize people with a "thank you" or "job well done" at the time they've done something you appreciate. However, if you do not have an opportunity to thank them at the moment, do so as you pass the flight attendant as you leave the plane, or comment to the head flight attendant to pass on your appreciation.

Using an Airplane Telephone and Fax/Data Transmission

You may find two types of telephones on airplanes today. The first airline telephone was the Airfone. If installed on the plane, they are typically located at the front of each cabin section. They work like any other U.S. telephone that takes a credit card. Airfones typically take the following credit cards: Visa, American Express, MasterCard, Discover, Diners Club, and the Air Travel Card.

The newer airline telephone is the Seatphone. These are typically located in the middle of a row of seats. With this portable airline telephone, you can reach it from your seat, and remain seated to make your call.

Calls can be made while flying over the contiguous U.S., most of Alaska, and within 200 miles of the U.S. coastline. The number of calls that may be placed at one time is limited. Ground to air service may not be available at all airports.

Complete in-flight calling instructions for placing a call from air to ground and for receiving a call from ground to air will be found on the unit. To receive ground to air calls you must register on each flight segment. Registration is free. You are billed only for calls you accept. Billing begins when a call is answered. Fractions of minutes are rounded to the next higher minute.

Rates for in-flight telephone calls are not inexpensive. For domestic, Canadian, and 800-number calls (including ground to air) the cost is $2.50 per call to connect plus $2.50 per minute, and applicable taxes. International calls are $5 per call to connect plus $5 per minute plus taxes. Rates for all operator-assisted calls are available upon request. The liability of the air carrier and the telephone company for failure of communications transmission is limited to call charges only.

Fax/data transmission is also possible on some flights. You will need to consult a flight attendant regarding use and any restrictions. The use of electronic devices, such as laptop computers is subject to Federal Aviation Administration (FAA) regulations and airline policy. If you are allowed to transmit data you will need to be sure your communications software has the recommended modem speed, and that you have programmed the correct delay before transmission begins. For best results, fax three or fewer pages.

AIRPORT SERVICES

Many more services than you ever thought possible are available at major airports for business travelers. So, if you are in need of a particular service, check to see if it is available before assuming it isn't.

Meet-and-greet services at the airport can include airport assistance in the form of transportation, advance boarding passes and check-in, and curb-to-gate assistance. For groups, this service can include coordinating details with suppliers, food and beverage, and luggage handling. These firms also work with many local ground transportation companies in arranging sedans, limousines, luxury vans, and motor coaches.

Other services provided by these firms at the airport can include interpreters and multilingual guides, currency-exchange assistance, tours, spouse programs, shopping guides, and experienced travel staff available to assist any group in reaching any location. Conference and meeting rooms are now also becoming available at airports, as are offices available for rent for as little as an hour or for as long as an entire day. Though many airline clubs are nice, these other meeting room services offer you more privacy. Secretarial services, personal computers, fax machines, and overnight courier services also are available for your convenience at many airports. A businessperson can fly into the airport, conduct her business, and fly to her next destination without even leaving the airport.

WOMEN TRAVELING ALONE

A woman traveling alone should always take extra precautions to ensure her personal safety. A Washington, D.C., travel agency says, "Do everything you can to be safe."

Arrange a Pick-up

Yes, arrange a pick-up. Phone your hotel ahead of time to inquire whether they have airport pick-up service. If they do not, ask what cab fare to the hotel should be. This tip could save you money.

Skycaps and Bellhops

Save your energy for your presentations. Take advantage of the services available by allowing skycaps and bellhops to move your boxes, luggage, and other gear. Depending on the service received, consider tipping $1 for each box or bag.

Room Registration

Whenever you check into a room, the desk clerk usually says your room number aloud. When you check in, ask the clerk to write down your room number instead. For security, some hotels are starting to do this more often, but since most do not, be sure to ask right away to have your room number written down.

Room Location

Believe it or not, asking for a room near the elevator can be safer. Many people don't want a room near the elevator because these rooms are often noisy. Since they can be safer than farther down a very long, empty corridor, rooms near the elevator are something you may want to consider.

Entering Your Room

Always use caution when traveling alone. Have the porter enter your room first on arrival. So if anyone is in the room, the porter will be the first one to have to deal with the problem. While the porter is still in the room, look around. Quickly check through the room, in the closets, in the bathroom, and behind the curtains.

Intrusions

If someone who appears to be from the hotel knocks on your door with complimentary room service or is a maintenance person wanting to check something, ask him to wait a minute. Before you open the door, call the front desk to ask if the hotel has sent someone. Don't ever let anyone into your room until you have first checked on his legitimacy.

Returning to Your Room

Some women who travel often enter their room by saying something like, "Hi Jim, I'm back." Of course, they do this only if someone suspicious looking follows them down a deserted hotel corridor. Even though they say this feels silly, it works.

Fire Exit

After checking out your room, locate the nearest fire stairs. Keep your robe at the end of your bed. Put your watch, jewelry, money, and room key right next to your bed. If there is a fire, you can grab these items and run.

Hotel Door Locks

Hotel door locks are sometimes flimsy. If possible, prop a chair or a briefcase against the door. If someone does try to get in, it will take more time and will make more noise, so you will have more time to take action.

Dining Alone

When you must dine alone, take a book or newspaper with you and ask for a table for one. If you look busy, you are less likely to be bothered. You might also consider giving the maitre d' a tip, perhaps $5, and let him know you do not want to be bothered. Maitre d's usually are very good at looking after people who are alone.

Valet Parking

Most parking garages are no place to be alone, so use valet parking whenever it is available. Still, before you leave your car for valet parking, be sure to get a receipt. Stealing cars parked in valet lots is common.

22 International Etiquette

EUROPE

When traveling in Europe, many people don't worry as much about their manners as they do when traveling in a country such as Japan. Why is this so? Because manners and acceptable social behavior in Europe are so similar to those in the United States. But when it comes to most Americans and their manners abroad, similar is not sufficient. Most Europeans strive to keep alive their cultural heritage, a fact we must respect to be successful in our business dealings abroad.

If your European associate is to consider you competent, you must put your best foot forward. Being improperly dressed, innocently using mannerisms considered rude, and departing from local custom will detract from your image, and consequently from your business acumen in the eyes of Europeans.

Greetings

When greeting a European male, extend your hand for a handshake, just as you would when greeting an American. When greeting a woman, however, wait for her to extend her hand to you. Show the same deference to all people older than yourself, as all Europeans do.

This includes waiting for an elderly person to extend his hand for a handshake, rising when he enters a room, letting him start your conversation, and addressing him formally. Acceptable manner requires that you address everyone you meet formally, not just the elderly. Use business and social titles until you know people on a more personal basis or until they indicate that it's okay for you to address them by their first name. Also be sure to use formal salutations and closings in all correspondence. Any time you are unsure about how to greet or address someone, be formal and you'll be safe.

Dining

One area of etiquette in which European and American manners are essentially the same is that of dining. There are a few minor differences, though. One is that Europeans eat using the Continental style. When using this style, hold your fork in your left hand and your knife in your right. You then eat with your fork still in your left hand. The fork and knife should remain in your hands at all times. Use the Continental style only if you are comfortable with it.

Another difference is that Europeans tend to be somewhat more strict about table manners than Americans are. At no time during the meal should you rest your elbows on the table. However, both your hands need to be above the table at all times. To accomplish this, rest your wrists on the edge of the table.

During the meal, whether you're a guest in someone's home or dining in a restaurant, never tilt your chair back on two legs. Another mannerism Europeans frown on is the American tendency to push food onto a fork with a finger. You will also find that meals, even informal family ones, are most often still served in courses, a practice that is all but extinct in the United States. Wine is the beverage that accompanies the majority of your afternoon and evening meals. Sometimes you are offered a cheese course before dessert. And the last course, which consists of coffee or tea, depending upon which European country you're in, follows dessert. After-dinner drinks are frequently served after coffee.

The president of a medical products firm who has traveled internationally for business for over a decade says that when you are asked, "What would you like to eat?" ask, "What do you recommend?" As she says, "Asking what they would recommend gets you out of a lot of trouble before dinner and actually helps you start a conversation with your business associates." Also be willing to experiment by trying different foods.

European breakfasts are usually buffets with meats, cheeses, and hard rolls. Although business associates or clients are usually entertained in fine restaurants, having dinner at someone's home is a very personal, festive event, and you can plan on spending at least two to four hours there. Bringing gifts to the woman of the house is appropriate, but only flowers and chocolates are acceptable. For the man of the house, wine or cigars are appropriate gifts. When entertaining in the United States, it is customary for the host to show her guests around her home. This simply is not done in Europe. You should, however, compliment your host's home, even though you will only see one or two rooms. If you are entertaining an associate or client in a restaurant, be sure to place them facing the room instead of with their backs to the room.

Be aware that beer or wine is most often served at lunch. A light alcoholic beverage, such as sherry or champagne, is often served before dinner. Even though your host may urge you to begin eating as soon as you are served, never begin eating until everyone else's plate is filled. Helping yourself to seconds is considered improper in Europe. Ask your host for an additional serving, but let her finish her meal before doing so. And always compliment her on a fine meal. It's impolite to leave the table during the meal without first asking permission. It's best not to leave the table at all until your host gets up, which signals the end of the meal. Most of the time, guests are asked to move to the living room for a liqueur, or in France, an aperitif. After you've enjoyed your after-dinner drink, it is then time to leave.

If you have been entertained in a restaurant by a male business associate and the dinner included wives, it is appropriate to send flowers to the host the next day. Red roses are a standard gift.

Social Graces

In all European countries, chewing gum, cleaning your fingernails, and picking your teeth are all regarded as exceedingly rude. The German-born director of corporate planning for the Monsanto Company emphasized that picking one's teeth is considered the worst American custom of all. If you must clean your teeth, do it privately—in the rest room. The same businessman also mentioned that German children are taught a saying early on: "Wenn Du denkst Du bist allein, dann mache Deine Nägel rein," which means, "If you think you are alone, clean your nails." The point is that it is considered very rude to clean your nails in public, and so it should be done only when alone.

Business Matters

You can bet that since some of the world's leading fashion designers hail from Europe, your appearance had better be professional as well as stylish. Businesspeople recommend dressing in business attire at all times, even for evening meals. This is true for women as well as men. Businessmen: If you do not own a high-quality, fashionable suit, invest in one and take a few extra moments to polish your shoes, checking for worn soles or holes. Maintain a subdued, understated style of dress, and do not wear bright colors. If your white shirts are crisply pressed and accompanied by just the right ties and your hair is kept neatly trimmed, you'll be set. Businesswomen: Wear a suit and blouse, but a skirt and jacket—not pants—is the rule. Pants and sleeveless dresses are fine to wear around the house, but they are not to be seen in public.

Europeans are proud of their heritage and have some of the most famous art museums and musical events in the world. As a guest in Europe, don't be surprised if you are asked to attend such an event. But know how to dress properly for it. Most European artistic, dramatic, and musical events call for formal attire—preferably a tuxedo. For men, a dark suit will suffice if you forget to bring your dinner jacket. Women should wear a black cocktail dress.

When discussing business matters, be careful not to let your civic chauvinism show. That is, do not boast about the supremacy of

America and all things American. You should, however, know a good deal about American current events. Most Europeans are extremely well informed about American culture and politics.

Making telephone calls in European countries can be very expensive because of high hotel surcharges, often four to five times the cost of the call. A phone call can cost more than a room for the night. Hotels levy incredible surcharges. Just a few calls may cost $300 to $400. Europeans will tell you not to make phone calls from your hotel and tell you to use the post office phones. Post office phones have a meter and you pay for the call right then, and you get a receipt right away. The countries that businesspeople immediately mention as having the "most expensive telephone charges" from their hotels are Great Britain, Germany, and Holland.

Faxing has also become very common around the world. Most hotels throughout Europe now offer facsimile service, which is fast and sometimes cheaper than a long phone call. You may want to check with your hotel to see if sending a fax may be more cost effective than making a telephone call. However, be sure to check; sometimes it is very reasonable, but at other times large surcharges are added to this service too.

Most Europeans take their vacations in August. It is best not to plan visits for business during this time, unless it is a big conference.

Transportation

Throughout European countries, taxis are more prevalent and less expensive than in the United States. Most businesspeople choose to use taxis for the convenience. Only if they are on a fixed budget and have more open time schedules do they use the buses or subways.

GERMANY

Greetings and Social Graces

With reunification, the German people have again become one. It's wise to remember, though, that although some customs and courtesies are similar in the eastern and western parts of Germany, some are not.

Generally a friendly people, Germans are still more reserved than Americans. Always shake hands when greeting and departing, and extend your hand to women before men. If one's hand is dirty, the person may offer an elbow or forearm to be shaken. When in a group, do not cross your handshake over someone else's. If you are introduced to several people in the room it is usual to shake hands with everyone present. *Guten Tag!* (Good day!) is the most common greeting. A simple *Hallo* (Hello) is also used. English is usually understood, but many natives appreciate visitors who attempt to learn German.

When addressing strangers, acquaintances or colleagues, one combines a person's professional title with *Herr* (Mr.), *Frau* (Mrs.), *Fräulein* (Miss), or other titles and the last name. The titles can also be used without the name. For example, a male professor with a doctorate degree is addressed as *Herr Professor Doktor*; a female head of a department in business or government could be addressed as *Frau Direktorin*.

Punctuality is essential in Germany. Arriving late is seen not so much as a sign of rudeness, but as a lack of self discipline and as an indicator of unreliability. When arriving at someone's home for a meal or gathering, guests usually bring flowers—either unwrapped, or wrapped in cellophane—to the host. Paper is also an acceptable wrapping, but foil is not. In the western part of Germany, roses (symbols of love) and carnations (symbols of mourning) are avoided for business occasions. It is courteous to stand when your host arrives or joins a room and to remain standing until offered a seat again. It is also courteous to stand when a women enters a room. Not everyone adheres to these rules of etiquette, but it is polite to do so. Refreshments are almost always served to guests, even during short visits. Germans enjoy getting together for social occasions, but visits should be announced or arranged in advance.

Dress carefully when visiting prospective clients or business contacts in Germany. The way one dresses is seen as an expression of one's attitudes and opinions. German people follow Western dress, but it is wise to be as conservative and neat as possible when going out in public. A well-cut suit is a must for most business meetings. Dressing too casually or sloppily is inappropriate, and short-sleeved dress shirts are never worn. Wrinkled trousers and a sports jacket (let alone dirty shoes!) may not be attributed to a long journey, but interpreted as inefficiency and unreliability. Wear jewelry and cosmetics conservatively. And for those of you who carry pens in your front shirt pocket, leave them at home; this is also considered inappropriate.

Some American gestures are considered inappropriate in Germany. For example, in western Germany, pointing your index finger to your head is considered rude; you indicate that another person does not possess normal intelligence.

Europeans practice professional etiquette much more than American businesspeople do. Do not place your feet on any desk, chair, or table. Be respectful and professional by treating people and their belongings with respect. Call ahead to confirm or cancel appointments. When talking with another person, remove your hands from your pockets, as leaving them in is considered disrespectful. It almost goes without saying, then, that jingling the change in your pants pockets is considered rude.

When conversing with the German people, remember that they are usually well educated and often critically receive ideas different from their own. Because of their heritage in music, history, and art, they appreciate someone who can talk about these subjects. Germans can be critical of U.S. policies, but they do not generally dislike Americans. Most Germans, it seems, value hard work, order, and skill.

Note that in the German business world only the written word is legally binding. A 'gentlemen's agreement' can only be seen as a first step in the negotiations and any written contracts and agreements need to be checked meticulously by both parties involved.

Dining

Germans do not find it easy to mix business and private life and tend to entertain business clients mainly in hotels and restaurants. Only after several meetings, if one gets on well privately as well as in business, and indeed at top management level if a big business deal is being negotiated, an invitation to a private home is extended, usually to an evening meal. Note, however, that if you want to sell something to a German company it is you who are expected to do the entertaining, i.e. to extend an invitation to a restaurant and to pay for meals etc.

In Germany, as with other European countries, you can eat Continental style, with the fork in the left hand and the knife in the right. Still, it is fine to eat American style. Businesspeople think it helps let people know you are an American and your hosts will often be more helpful.

Do not cut your fish or potatoes with a knife, as this suggests to your host that they are not fully cooked. The custom of not using a knife in this way originated when knives were made of a material that stained when cutting potatoes and the stain could not be removed. To take care of the problem, your host often provides a fish knife. In Germany it is considered wasteful to leave food on your plate. Expect beer, wine, or mineral water with your meals, for tap water is seldom served. Soft drinks and fruit juices are also favorite beverages, but don't ask for ice. Germans do not consider iced drinks healthful.

In restaurants, how you pay for your drinks and meal varies based on the sophistication of the restaurant. In finer restaurants, the tip is usually included in the bill, and the server is paid at the table. Even when the tip is included, many round the total tab to the next mark and add the extra to the server's tip. In eastern Germany, tipping was illegal during communist reign but is no longer banned. In less formal establishments, servers often make scratch marks on your cardboard coaster under your drink as you order; then the server totals the marks and scratches the total on a piece of paper. Since he carries a money bag, you are able to pay the server and he can make change right at the table. Then you can tip him on the spot. If served by the restaurant owner, it is inappropriate to leave a tip.

Germany is famous for its sausages, a large variety of breads and cakes, and cold meats, so don't be surprised if you're treated to a meal that has these foods. Many parts of Germany have different "specialties." The "locals" are often impressed if you eat the local food. Be sure to ask because it is usually the best food in the restaurant. An example is the "White sausage" in Munich. The midday or main meal of the day usually includes soup, a main dish, and dessert. The evening meal in a restaurant is generally a full meal. The German people also favor potatoes, noodles, dumplings, sauces, vegetables, cakes, and pastries.

Business Matters

Before unification, business hours were different, and not all differences have been resolved. Shops in the east were open late to accommodate working spouses, while stores in the west closed by 6:30 P.M. It may be some time before a uniform system is developed. Business hours range from 8:00 A.M. to 5:00 P.M. weekdays. In western states, shops close at 2:00 P.M. on Saturdays, except one Saturday each month when they remain open into the evening. Banks close for lunch and then at 4:00 P.M., but they remain open a bit later on Thursdays.

Transportation

Public transportation is efficient for daily travel in major cities, so even though most families own cars; subways, buses, streetcars, and trains form the main transportation network. This is due to heavy traffic and limited parking. Trains travel to nearly every town and city. Traffic rules are carefully obeyed by drivers and cyclists. One must attend expensive and rigorous driver training schools to qualify for a driver's license. While there is no speed limit on sections of the *Autobahn* (freeway) in western states, there are strict limits on all other roads.

GREAT BRITAIN

Greetings and Social Graces

To prepare yourself for a trip to Great Britain, remember every little tidbit about manners you ever learned, heard or read. Being on your absolute best behavior is necessary, because formality and propriety are expected in everything you do, but especially in business matters. You can begin your semi-casual American behavior again only after you receive an invitation from your host to do so. However, this does not give you license to slap someone on the back, put your arms around her shoulder, or give a two-handed handshake. Physical contact of this nature is unacceptable. In fact, physical contact in general and demonstrative hand gestures are both limited. Even handshakes are given only when you meet someone and on formal occasions. Handshakes are generally firm but not aggressive. When people are already acquainted, verbal greetings are often used instead. Among friends, women are often kissed (by men and women) lightly on both cheeks. When passing a stranger on the street, it is appropriate to smile and say "Good morning," "Hello, " "Good afternoon," or "Good evening," if eye contact is established with that person. Young people and friends are called by their first name, but titles (Mr., Mrs., Doctor, etc.) are used in formal situations or to show respect.

Being loud and boisterous in public or in private conversation (except in very informal gatherings) gives your British counterparts the impression that you conduct business in the same unpleasant manner. The English are in general a reserved people. Personal space is respected, and people feel uncomfortable when someone stands too close to them during conversation. Touch is generally avoided. Also simple, everyday conversation starters in the United States aren't appropriate in Britain. Asking someone what he does for a living or how much he paid for something is no way to begin a conversation. Stay away from personal questions, politics, royal family gossip, and religion. Saying please and thank you is necessary for even the smallest gesture, so be sure to say them often. Send handwritten thank you's to accept a dinner invitation, and always display proper table manners. And even if you are extravagantly wealthy, don't make it apparent when you're in Britain. Doing so will make an impression on others—but it will not be a favorable one.

You might think that because the British speak English, you'll have no trouble communicating with them, because their vocabulary words have the same meanings as those used in America. English is English, correct? Sorry, but no. We might use the same words and phrases, but they don't all mean the same thing. When a British person says he is going to take the tube to work, he is referring to the subway. Another confusing word is *pants*. When an American refers to pants as an article of clothing, we know he means slacks, jeans, or trousers. But when a British person refers to his pants, he is talking about underclothing. *Suspenders* mean "garters." The British have a number of words that are not used at all in the United States. To save yourself and others needless embarrassment, get an English-American dictionary and familiarize yourself with its content before you leave the United States.

Business Matters

In business, the rules are simple: Mind your own business, keep your mind on business, and don't be late. In other words, don't invade your British counterpart's privacy by asking personal questions, glancing over his shoulder to see what he's working on, or straying off onto business topics other than the one you came to discuss. Refrain from telling him the latest details of your personal life, no matter how exciting they may be, unless you want to embarrass him or make him uncomfortable. Be willing to listen as well as speak, but lavishing your British associate with compliments isn't going to get you anywhere. However, showing that you are concerned about the matter at hand and that you can keep confidential information will. Showing an interest in British politics, religion, and influence in the world and having enough knowledge of them to hold a conversation will help you hold your audience's attention. If you do give a speech or presentation, introduce yourself briefly and be available for questions afterwards. And no matter what happens, do not be late for any appointment. Businesspeople say the British are not very punctual, even though they have this reputation. They say most of them go by "ish" time, such as "sevenish."

Particularly in Great Britain, presidents of companies are called managing directors. The presidential title doesn't carry as much clout or prestige there as it does in the United States, unless you are a president of a large company. In fact, in Britain the title has a rather negative connotation. To prevent your British business associates from thinking negatively of you if you are the president of a company, leave your presidential title at home and introduce yourself as the managing director while in Europe. You might even reprint your business cards for the trip.

Business discussions are confined to the length of the workday— 9:00 A.M. to 5:00 P.M., Monday through Friday. Business stays at the office; it doesn't come home with you in the evening and it isn't the topic of weekend or dining conversations. You'll find that because of the heavy traffic and lack of sufficient parking, most businesspeople take the tube to work. Once in the city, walking or taking a cab is the best way to go. If you do venture out for a walk, be sure to take a good map, and remember your umbrella.

If you're going to be calling or mailing documents to your office in the United States, mailing documents to Britain before you get there, or sending messages elsewhere while in Britain, know something about the phone and mail service in Great Britain. When doing business over the phone, keep in mind that calls are least expensive after 6:00 P.M., but rates are also discounted between 8:00 A.M. and 9:00 A.M. and after 1:00 P.M. If you're calling from a hotel, brace yourself for the rather large service charge that will be added to your bill. This is true in most European countries. You may save money by making international calls directly from public phones. You can also get debit phone cards from post offices and news agents. Another option is to send a telegram, known as a *telemessage*, which is delivered the next day (Monday through Saturday) if your message is in by 10:00 P.M. Sending something to Great Britain from the United States or to the United States from Great Britain via DHL Worldwide Express service takes one or two business days, and two via Federal Express. Mail sent within Great Britain normally arrives the next business day. The post office also offers its own express service.

If you don't own any conservative clothing, this is the time to add some to your wardrobe. Nothing less than a dark colored, three-piece, pinstriped, and finely tailored suit is acceptable. And do not go wearing all of your gold jewelry. Not only will you look terribly out of place, but you won't be trusted by your British business associates.

Dining and Visiting

You may find that you'll have time on your hands in the evenings to go sightseeing or otherwise entertain yourself, because even though the British are more likely than any other Europeans to invite you to their home, this doesn't necessarily mean they do it often. Don't be offended by this or get the impression that the British don't like to entertain, though. It's actually done (or not done) out of respect for you, because they don't want to intrude on your privacy in the evening. Thus, they do the majority of their business entertaining during lunch. On the one extreme, business entertaining may consist of eating at an inexpensive local pub, or on the other extreme, dining at one of Britain's expensive fine restaurants. When dining, you may eat in the American style, even though the British use the Continental. Of course, remember your table manners. When in a restaurant, raising your hand is the best way to get a server's attention, and he will bring your bill on a plate on which you also leave a 10 percent tip.

If you are invited to your business associate's home for dinner, it's best to be precisely on time, but if you can't be, it's better to be a few minutes late than a few minutes early. Be sure to bring a small gift such as flowers or chocolate for your hostess, and return the hospitality by inviting your host and hostess out to dinner or to the theater. If you make social calls or go visiting, be sure to call ahead of time and bring a small gift for the hostess. A smile and handshake are appropriate when greeted at the door. Your British hostess will enjoy your company even more if you show an interest in and knowledge of her country's history and culture and are able to converse about such subjects. Remember to offer to pay for any phone calls you make from her home, as even local calls are billed.

Many people associate Great Britain with tea, a reasonable association to make. But not all tea is tea, just as not all English is English, at least as those in America know it. The first thing you need to know about drinking tea in Britain is that it is going to be served very strong and with milk. When you are invited for "high tea," you will be served sandwiches and possibly fruitcake in a semiformal fashion during the late afternoon. Late afternoon is also the time for "cream tea," which is tea accompanied by whipped cream-filled pastry (cream cakes) or biscuits with clotted cream and preserves (scones). "Time for tea" means that it's time for supper. Tea is served only until the late afternoon or until their supper at the latest. After this, only coffee is served. "White coffee" is coffee with milk or cream added.

Transportation

When in Great Britain, you can travel by bus, taxi, subway, or car. Bus fare is paid either upon entering the bus or when the conductor collects it. When the bus is full, men surrender their seats to women and the elderly. Raising your hand high in the air is the standard way to flag a taxi, and cab drivers get a 10 percent tip. The subway, or the Underground as it is better known, is the quickest way to get from one place to another in the London metropolitan area. Before you ride the Underground, you must visit the ticket office to purchase tickets, which are collected once you reach your destination. If you decide to drive while in Great Britain, don't forget that the British drive on the left side of the road, and the "round abouts" can be a real trick. Also, these "round abouts" are important to remember when walking around. Be sure to look both ways before stepping off the curb. Traveling in Great Britain is generally rather quick and easy.

FRANCE

Greetings

When in France, it is important to keep on your toes as far as manners and etiquette are concerned. The French are not very patient with a visitor's rudeness or ignorance of their ways, although they do appreciate visitors who try to speak French and will generally help them with pronunciation and translation. If you aren't fluent in French and don't have the luxury of traveling with a translator, the best way to establish good relations with and show respect for your French business associate is to apologize for not being able to speak or understand her language.

Introductions, scheduled appointments, and written confirmations of them, and being referred to a new business contact are all "musts" when doing business in France. You don't just stroll into an office and say that you'd like to speak to an executive of the company without having an appointment and without being referred to her by someone she knows and trusts. Nothing short of a formal introduction is acceptable, and she is always addressed by her formal title, preceded by "Monsieur" or "Madam," unless she indicates that it's acceptable for you to do otherwise. Members of her staff are also addressed by their formal titles. Shake your associate's hand when you leave as well as when your greet her. This isn't the usual American handshake, though. Keep your grip light, and give a quick single shake when giving a French handshake. An aggressive handshake is considered impolite. In France, men still traditionally extend their hands to women, and those with high rank, superior authority, or an official position offer to shake the hands of visitors. Shaking a Frenchperson's arm or elbow is not out of line if his or her hands are dirty. Touching cheeks and "air kissing" is common among close friends and young people.

Social Graces

Gestures and social habits aren't as relaxed in France as they are in the United States. Thus, unless you pay attention to your behavior, you may find that exhibiting many of your everyday American behaviors is going to get you some questioning or disapproving looks from the French. In the United States, slapping your open hand over your closed fist can have a variety of meanings, but in France it carries a vulgar connotation and should be avoided. If you want to gesture "okay" with your hands while in France, give the American "thumbs up" sign; otherwise, the French will interpret your gesture as "zero." When talking with someone, it's rude to have your hands in your pockets or to chew gum in public. When seated, one's knees must be together, or one leg can be crossed over the other knee. One always sits erect, and never with your feet on tables or chairs. Toothpicks, nail clippers, and combs should never be used in public. If you must sneeze or blow your nose, do it quietly so you don't draw attention to yourself, and be sure to use a handkerchief or tissue. And no matter how tired you are or how badly you itch, don't yawn or scratch in public.

Business Matters

Businesses and non-food shops open from 9:00 or 9:30 A.M. to 6:00 or 6:30 P.M., Monday through Saturday. Some large stores stay open until 9:00 P.M. one or two evenings a week. Small shops, especially in rural towns, may close for lunch and on Mondays. Many food shops open as early at 7:00 A.M. and on Sunday mornings. Banks close at 4:30 P.M. Many businesses close on holidays. The average workweek is 39 hours.

The communications system is modern. You will pay high service charges for calls made at hotels and many restaurants, so make international calls from public phones. Pay phones generally use phone cards (*telecarte*) purchased at a post office. They are based on time used and can be used more than once—until the time paid for runs out. The post office is the center for various forms of communications and transactions. If you make a call from a post office, be sure you have money with you so you're able to pay for it when you're done. Sending items by DHL Worldwide Express from the United States to France will take one to two days, two by Federal Express, but Federal Express doesn't service Corsica. Items sent from France reach their American destination in one to two days via DHL, and in two to three via Federal Express. France also has its own express delivery system, Chronopost, which promises next-day delivery within the country.

Because the French do take their work so seriously, they don't rush into any agreements. This means that you must exercise great patience. Be thorough in your presentation or explanation, and base it only on the most accurate and current information, because it will be closely scrutinized. And you would be wise to sharpen your negotiation and communication skills. The French are also firm believers of putting and receiving everything in writing, and all correspondence should, of course, be formal and written in correct French. Pay close attention to your body language and facial expressions. The French are very keen observers of nonverbal communication.

Formal and *conservative* are the key words to remember when packing business attire for a trip to France. The French in general take great care to dress well and fashionable, whether they are wearing formal or casual attire, and they feel more at ease with visitors who show the same degree of attention to appearance. Paris is the home of many of the world's leading fashion designers. Men will definitely get their money's worth out of tailored dark suits, white shirts, and fashionable ties. A businessman is expected to always wear a tie. Women's outfits should be conservative, professional, formal, and simple. And their outfits must include skirts, not pants. Wearing pants or other casual clothing to business appointments and engagements is unthinkable. In southern France, attire can be more casual but not less stylish, and no matter what the occasion, both men and women must be neatly and tastefully dressed.

Dining and Visiting

You're not likely to receive an invitation to your French business associate's home, because the French, like the British, usually do all their business entertaining in restaurants. Your host will be more than happy to select an item from the menu for you, and always be sure to compliment the cuisine and savor the wine by sipping it. It is French custom to serve the salad after the entrée. In France, one of the most important components of a meal is the sauce served with it; it should never be left on your plate. Most use their bread to soak it up. Remember that your bread should not be used as a shovel. And even though the dinner atmosphere may be relaxed, your table manners must not be. You should not be the one to bring up the subject of business over a meal. Your French associate will subtly approach it over dessert and coffee after she has gotten a chance to know you a little better. Don't forget that if you invite your associate out, the only acceptable restaurant is an expensive restaurant. And, the person who invites or makes the suggestion is the one who pays.

If, by chance, you are invited to an associate's home for dinner, bring a small bouquet of flowers (no roses (which express love) or chrysanthemums (used in cemeteries), a small box of fine chocolates for the host, or wine. Wine is consumed with most meals (except breakfast) and there are dozens of varieties. The French know the difference between fine wine and poorer varieties. Unless certain of its high quality, foreign guests should not give wine as a gift. Guests usually arrive on time because punctuality is a sign of courtesy. However, for some social events it is also polite to arrive a few minutes late— to allow the hosts extra time for final preparations. Wait for your host to ask you in and take your coat. He will also show you to your seat. You are likely to be offered a drink before dinner, but it's acceptable to ask for a nonalcoholic beverage instead. Conversing over dinner is fine as long as you don't ask personal questions or talk about money or politics. The hosts should be complimented on the meal; good cooking is a matter of pride in French homes. Wait for a break in the conversation before ending your visit, and kindly thank your host. At the door, small talk, expressions of thanks, and repeated goodbyes continue; it is impolite to be in a hurry to leave. A thank-you note is often sent the day after one has been a dinner guest.

The French also use the Continental style of eating, but you may still use the American. Etiquette is important. Both hands remain above the table at all times. A man may rest his wrists, and a woman her forearms, on the table edge. Elbows are not placed on the table. It is impolite to speak with food in the mouth. It is improper to help oneself twice to cheese. Some foods are also eaten a little differently in France than they are in the United States. When served fruit, peel it with your knife before slicing and eating it with your fork. Big leaves of lettuce are not cut; they're folded into bite-sized pieces with your fork. Bread is broken with the fingers and used to wipe the plate. When not in use, forks and knives belong on the edge of your plate, not on the tablecloth. One places the knife and fork parallel across the plate when finished. Formal lunches and dinners may last more than two hours. And be warned: Some formal lunches and dinners have been known to consist of twelve courses (although a typical family meal has two to four courses).

Transportation

Traveling is not difficult in France. The public transportation system in Paris is among the world's finest. You can choose from the subway (called the Metro), buses, trains, and taxis, all of which are widely available. Buses serve most cities and train service extends to even the smallest towns. Trains are best for long distance travel. Most people own private cars, which are generally small French brands. Taxis in urban areas are expensive. Take into consideration, too, that taxi rates increase by 50 percent after 10:00 P.M. and that it's safer to take the subway during the day than at night. The French National Railroad is another option. It offers reasonably priced tours, is a quick means of transportation, and links Paris with many major French and European cities. The French domestic air system is efficient, and car ferries link France with Corsica and Great Britain. In 1994, a new rail link to England opened. A trip from Paris to London, crossing under the English Channel, takes three hours. The actual time in the tunnel is 35 minutes.

ITALY

Greetings and Social Graces

When meeting Italians, be prepared to be friendly, hospitable and warm, because that's how you will be greeted. Italians will do almost anything in their power to ensure that you feel welcome in their country. When being introduced to or greeting an Italian, be sure to address him by his formal title and don't forget to shake hands. Men, women, friends, and government officials all shake hands in greeting. If your hand is dirty, you may offer a forearm or finger instead, or simply apologize for not shaking hands. Titles carry much prestige and signify achievement, and handshakes signify trust. All of these are very important and must be recognized if you hope to have a successful business relationship with the Italians.

It is a must for guests to be introduced first, and the standard response to any introduction is "It's a pleasure to meet you." Italians say *Ciao* ("Hi" or "Goodbye") just as Americans do as an informal greeting to friends in public. Other terms include *Buon giorno* ("Good day") and *Buona sera* ("Good evening.") It is not unusual for two members of the same gender to walk arm in arm or for good friends to appear to greet each other with a kiss on both cheeks. Actually, friends touch cheeks and "kiss the air." Keep in mind when in public: If you must yawn or sneeze, be sure to cover your mouth.

Business Matters

The Italians have a different work schedule than most business-people in the United States. They work Monday through Friday, 8:00 or 9:00 A.M. to 1:00 P.M., have a break until 3:00 P.M. and then work until 6:00 P.M. or 7:00 P.M. Many Italians also work on Saturdays. Businesses are generally closed on Sunday. It is usually up to you, as a visitor, to find something to do during the extended lunch period. Grocery stores close one afternoon of the week and barber shops are closed on Mondays. Banks and government offices are generally open from 8:00 A.M. to 2:00 P.M. Italians celebrate most major Catholic holidays, as well as some national holidays. Celebrations honoring local patron saints vary according to region, and various festivals are also held throughout the year.

If you must make international calls when in Italy, it's easier to make them from phone centers and pay for them then, than it is to go through a hotel switchboard. And if you plan on using an Italian pay phone, know that they don't take regular coins, as American pay phones do. They operate only on tokens called *gettoni* which must be bought from a post office or tobacconist. Mail sent to Italy from the United States arrives there one to two business days later by DHL Worldwide Express, three to four by Federal Express. When mailing items from Italy to the U.S. via DHL, allow two business days. To send mail to the United States by Federal Express, contact their Italian agent, Saimex, at telephone number 6-622-1551.

Whereas the French are very adamant about correspondence and getting all details in writing, Italians generally are not. The Italian business lifeline is the telephone, because the Italian postal service is at times not reliable.

Knowing the Italian language, even a few words, is advantageous when dealing with Italian businesspeople. Your conversation will flow more smoothly if you avoid the heated topics of religion and politics and stick to soccer, local news, business, and family matters. And be prepared to wait for Italians to make decisions regarding business. They, too, don't rush into or make any hasty decisions and are also likely to run into bureaucratic delays. Also know that it's important to be on time for any and all appointments. But when in Rome, you're likely to get stuck in traffic, and saying that you were (only when you really were!) is an acceptable excuse for being late.

Italians pride themselves on always being well dressed. Business attire is conservative, but at the same time it's elegant. How you're dressed is very important. A very finely tailored suit, white shirt, and tie are appropriate for men. Women are expected to wear professionally and fashionably coordinated outfits of dresses and blazers or skirts and blouses. Other appearance reminders: Italians seldom wear worn or dirty clothing, they don't walk around barefoot or in stocking feet in public, and they don't venture out in public unless they're completely dressed. Doing any of the preceding will lead others to believe that you're very impolite. It's inappropriate to wear dark glasses indoors, and men should always remove their hats when greeting others and entering buildings.

Dining and Visiting

Only after your relationship has progressed from business to one of a more personal nature are you likely to be invited to your Italian counterpart's home for dinner. This is one dinner invitation you cannot turn down, as it would be an insult to your host. It is recommended that you present your host with a gift, such as flowers, a wrapped box of chocolates, or wine. If you do decide on flowers, they should not be chrysanthemums or calla lilies because these are used only to decorate graves. Tradition also dictates that you bring an odd number of flowers.

The Italians also eat in the Continental style, but you may eat in the American style. Dinner is a leisurely affair that can last anywhere from one to four hours. Conversing over dinner is acceptable, and some topics you may want to bring up are soccer, politics, family affairs, business, and local events/news. Showing some interest in your host's children is also very polite, as family is very important to Italians. Complimenting everything from the meal, your host's home to her children is much appreciated. Even if you don't like one of the dishes, eat a small portion of it anyway. During the meal, a person's hands are kept above the table; to have hands in the lap is improper. At the table, it is impolite to stretch, even if the meal is over. Eat your dessert with a teaspoon or fork, and place your silverware parallel to each other on your plate when you're finished. Remain seated at the table until everyone has finished eating. There's no need for you to feel obligated to help clear the table or do the dishes after dinner as guests do not volunteer to help clean up.

Breakfast in Italy is very light, usually a cup of coffee, *biscotti* cookies, and a roll. Lunch is the main meal of the day and is eaten around 1:00 P.M. Typically it includes three courses: pasta, fish, or another meat with vegetables, and fruit. In Italian restaurants, you order either soup or pasta; one does not eat both in the same meal. Pasta is ordered as an appetizer and is followed by a meat dish. Meat is not automatically served with rice or other side dishes, as it normally is in the United States. Anything you would like to have with your meat dish needs to be ordered separately. Remember that salad is served after the entrée, because it is thought to cleanse the palate. And Italian dinner is lighter than lunch. You will be able to order cappuccino and other milk coffees only until 10:00 A.M. Black coffee is served the rest of the day. Wine is a common drink and is widely used in cooking. Italian pizza is not the same as American pizza and is different in various regions of Italy. When eating at restaurants, a service charge is often included in the bill, but it is appropriate to also leave a small tip for the waiter.

Transportation

You will be able to travel around Italy by bus, train, or taxi. Buses and trains are the principal means of public transportation and are both inexpensive and known for departing and arriving on schedule. Taxis are another option. There is the less expensive metered variety and the unmetered, which you'd do best to avoid. The public transportation system in general is up to date and a reliable means of transportation. Unfortunately, one can't say the same about road travel, which tends to be unstable and unpredictable. Care should be taken in some larger cities against car thieves and pickpockets. As in every major city, it is not a good idea to keep valuables in the the car. In addition to ground travel, Rome and Milan are serviced by many major international airlines.

JAPAN

You may one day find yourself working with Japanese businesspeople. Be sure to learn Japanese customs so you can understand them.

In the past, Japanese wives were not typically brought to business dinners. However the times are changing. Today, it depends on the situation. Japan is becoming much more Westernized. Japanese businesswomen are mostly found in clerical and accounting staff positions, unless they are the wife of the business owner or own their own business. Japanese businessmen do respect businesswomen from the United States.

Language

The Japanese won't expect you to know their language. It is very complex, and although it includes only a few dialects, there are many different accents. Still, the Japanese appreciate visitors who attempt to speak their language. If nothing else, you may be providing inexpensive entertainment for your hosts!

Avoid using slang, jargon, and idioms. The Japanese may be fascinated by them, but few understand them. When talking to a Japanese person, speak slowly, and distinctly, and *not* loudly. Repeat a sentence two or three times if necessary, but do not raise your voice. They may not understand everything you're saying, but they'll say "hai" and nod in agreement. What they are really saying is, "I hear you," or "uh huh"; they are not necessarily agreeing with you. American businesspeople need to be very aware of this. It is a mistake to assume automatically that a Japanese person is agreeing with you. One Fortune 500 firm had many problems in finalizing some business transactions, since their employees were not aware of this.

The Japanese place great worth on nonverbal language or communication. For example, much can be said with a proper bow. In fact, one is often expected to sense another person's feelings on a subject without verbal communication. Westerners often misinterpret this as a Japanese desire to be vague or incomplete. The Japanese may consider a person's inability to interpret feelings as insensitivity.

Become familiar with what the Japanese really mean when they say something or make a gesture. What they say or do and what they mean often are not the same. Pressing for a commitment is offensive to the Japanese. Don't make the mistake of interpreting their words and actions as they would be interpreted in America. For instance, if your Japanese business associate expresses how difficult an issue is, he usually is saying no. If he crosses his arms, leans back, and closes his eyes after you tell him something, he's not bored or falling asleep; he's just thinking it over.

It is impolite to yawn in public. A person sits up straight with both feet on the floor. Legs may be crossed at the knee or ankles, but it is improper to place an ankle over a knee. Beckoning is done by waving all fingers with the palm down. It is polite to point with the entire hand. Shaking one hand from side to side with the palm forward means "no." A person refers to himself by pointing the index finger at his nose. Laughter does not necessarily signify joy or amusement; it can also be a sign of embarrassment. Chewing gum in public is considered impolite.

Be very honest when speaking with the Japanese, for they will take you at your word. Don't say you like raw fish if you don't because if you do you will be taken to a sushi house for dinner. Don't overly praise decorations, household equipment, or art objects when visiting a home; doing so implies that you would like to take them with you when you leave.

Social Graces

Avoid public displays of affection and do not physically touch the Japanese. To refuse something or say no, just say, "No thanks." When addressing others, it's always better to be more formal than not and to be very courteous in your business dealings. In general, take things slowly and watch your Japanese business associates carefully. They will often assist you with important social customs.

Never step on a tatami mat while wearing your shoes or slippers. The *tatami* is the straw mat that covers Japanese floors. You will most likely encounter tatami mats in restaurants and some homes.

Business Matters

The Japanese businessperson is very hard working. Their typical work week includes Saturday. It is not unusual to work six or seven days a week. Business hours in Japan are from 8:00 A.M. to 5:00 P.M., or 9:00 A.M. to 6:00 P.M., Monday through Friday, and from 9:00 A.M. until noon on Saturday. Banks and government offices have similar hours. Many Japanese work late into the evening; overtime is a common necessity. Even though Japanese businesspeople work long hours, when they are dining out don't expect them to talk business right away. Tea ceremonies, conversation on a variety of topics, and lengthy negotiation are common before any business matters are actually discussed. Remain very patient and wait for the formalities to end. Trying to rush the Japanese into making a business decision before they're ready isn't going to work. Being invited to participate in a tea ceremony is an honor. If you're unsure of how to behave, follow the host's example.

When making telephone calls in Japan, be sure to use the appropriately colored phone or you may never get in touch with anyone you want. For local calls, use the pink, red, or blue phone. When dialing long distance or internationally, use the green phones. Green phones work anywhere and take calling cards. The major Japanese cities have KDD phone centers from which you can place collect and international calls and send international telegrams. You can also send telegrams or faxes from post offices and railroad stations. It generally takes two to three business days for mail to reach Japan from the United States via DHL Worldwide Express, four to five days by Federal Express. Allow one to two business days for mail to reach the United States when sent from Japan via DHL, and three to four days via Federal Express. To contact Airway Express, the Federal Express agent in Japan, dial 2-732-0101. DHL express service is also available at most hotel business centers. To get mail to Japan within 48 hours, your best bet may be Express Mail through the U.S. post office.

Business Cards

Exchanging business cards is a formal ritual in Japan. The importance of the business card, or *meishi*, to the Japanese cannot be emphasized enough. They revere them and often keep every business card they ever receive in their lifetime. Business cards are honored and essential because the Japanese businessperson relies on them to find out another's social and business rank without asking. Knowing this rank is important because it establishes who is the higher ranking individual, sets the level of language to use, and provides information from which to start a conversation. But, do not include your college degree (e.g., M.B.A., Ph.D.) on your business card.

When going to Japan or any other country, have your cards printed in English on one side and in the language of the country you're traveling to on the other, but it is especially important in Japan. Many people who travel to Japan on business mail their card before they arrive so they can be translated and printed in Japanese. There are, however, many print shops in the United States that now provide this service. So you can present your card at your first meeting. Also make sure any information or sales brochures you bring to a meeting are already translated into that countries language.

When presenting your business card, hold your card facing up at the top two corners, then bow briefly. The other person gives you his business card simultaneously. Be sure to bow and accept it with both hands. Take time to read the card and verify the pronunciation, if you don't it's an insult. Do not write on the card. This American custom is considered offensive in Japan. It's improper to pass cards out or leave them fanned on tables. You need to either be introduced to your counterpart by someone who knows you both or send a letter of introduction to him before you arrive.

When in Japan, keep written records of and get written confirmation on all business matters. Let your host know of your itinerary and what you hope to accomplish on your trip before you arrive to make sure it's acceptable to him. Last and most important, be on time. The Japanese are very punctual. This means allowing more than enough time to travel between business appointments because you're almost certain to get stuck for long periods of time in traffic.

Bowing

A bow is the traditional greeting between Japanese. While some appreciate it when Westerners bow, others do not, especially when the two people are not acquainted. Therefore, a handshake is probably the most appropriate for foreign visitors. Be alert in each situation to determine whether to bow or shake hands. As an American businessperson, you do not have to bow. Still, bowing is a custom for which the Japanese are known, and it is a very important part of their culture. Although it is not as strongly enforced as it once was, bowing is still used in many forms of salutations. There are two main forms of bowing, the ordinary salutation and the slight bow. The ordinary salutation is a more respectful and formal bow than the light bow and can be made while sitting down or standing. While sitting place your palms four to six inches apart on the floor and bow quietly by lowering your head between your hands four to six inches from the floor. To bow while standing, stand straight and look straight ahead. Bow smoothly from your waist at about a 30 degree angle. Do not look up while you are bowing. Lower your hands to your knees, palms down, and lift your head after a short pause.

The light bow can be made while sitting or standing. The body is bent at the waist at about a 15 degree angle, and the hands may be lowered to the knees or left at the sides, if you are a man. Women are not to leave their hands at their sides; instead they press their palms together. This bow is normally made after the initial, acknowledging salutation is made.

Bowing is a sign of respect, and thus you bow anytime someone bows to you and when meeting others. Persons wishing to show respect or humility bow lower than the other person. Proper etiquette requires that you bow lower than the Japanese person, and the higher the Japanese person's rank, the lower you bow (within reason). Also avoid making too much eye contact; the Japanese find it offensive. Refrain from touching a Japanese person when you greet him in public. Handshakes are becoming more acceptable, but let your Japanese associate initiate it. Most Japanese businesspeople now shake hands. The Japanese are usually addressed by adding "san" to the end of their last name, in the same way that Mr. is used in North America. "Mr. Yamamoto" in the United States would be called "Yamamoto-san" in Japan. The use of first names is reserved for family and friends.

Visiting

Visits are usually arranged in advance; spontaneous visits are uncommon in urban areas. When visiting a home, it is Japanese custom to remove your scarf or hat and gloves at the door before ringing the bell. Present your business card or state your name after making a light bow to the person who answers the door. Upon entering the house, remove your shoes, using only your hand, and leave them facing the door. You may remove your coat either before or after you enter the house. If you leave your coat on because you are cold, apologize to your host. Slippers, if presented, are worn, and the host is followed into the room.

As a guest, you will be presented with a cushion on which to sit, but it is best not to seat yourself until you have greeted the host. In the winter, you may sit on the cushion before the host arrives, but sit on the tatami when greeting him. Greet him only after he has been seated. You may then return to the cushion at the host's request. When in business suits, men may ask permission to sit crosslegged on the tatami instead of in the traditional Japanese style. Women may point their feet out to the sides a little instead of sitting on them.

You are likely to be offered tea and cakes not only when visiting a home, but also when visiting a business. In Japan, the host is always the first to eat.

When leaving, bow and thank your host. Gather your scarf or hat, gloves, and coat, and remove the slippers so you can put on your shoes. Slippers are to be left facing away from the door. It is acceptable to put your coat on either before or after you leave the house.

Very little business entertaining is conducted in private homes, because Japanese homes are very small. Entertaining in restaurants is more common. Whether you must remove your shoes in a restaurant depends upon the restaurant. Be prepared to, just in case. This means always wearing socks without holes. Remember though, never step on a tatami with your shoes on, even in a restaurant.

Dining

Reservations are essential when dining at expensive restaurants in Japan. Tips are not given, yet fancy restaurants often add a 10 to 15 percent service charge to your check. Credit cards are most commonly accepted only in major American hotels and from people who are well known in a particular restaurant. If your Japanese counterpart offers to pay for your meal, let him. Just make sure you pay for the next one or treat him if he visits you in your country.

Eating

Eating a Japanese meal properly involves following a few rules of Japanese etiquette, but becoming familiar with them requires only a little practice. Always show your intention to begin eating and give a slight bow before starting your meal.

To be very polite, use both hands to put your rice bowl on the tray presented to you when you are served rice. Most men, though, usually use just one hand, which is fine also. Wait to begin eating your rice until you have placed your bowl back on the table or tray after it has been filled. Rice is eaten by holding the rice bowl flat on the fingers of your left hand while resting your thumb on the rim of the bowl for support. Typically the Japanese eat from their bowl while holding it at chest level instead of bending down to the table. Chopsticks, hashi are used to eat most meals, and are held in the right hand, although it is acceptable to use your left hand. People generally use Western utensils when eating Western food.

If you are at a formal tea ceremony, eat two or three mouthfuls of rice and set the rice bowl down. Pick up your soup bowl with your right hand and place it in the palm of your left. Drink some soup. After eating rice again, the soup or any other dish may be eaten. Pickles are always eaten last. Show that you have finished eating by leaving some rice in your bowl, replacing all the bowl covers, and placing your chopsticks on your tray.

Don't be surprised if you hear food and noodles being slurped. But no matter how rude or annoying slurping may seem to you, don't comment on it. It is common in Japan and it is not a violation of Japanese etiquette. If you use a toothpick in a Japanese restaurant, be sure to cover your mouth with your hand.

Gifts

Japan is a very gift-oriented country. Be prepared to give and receive gifts. The gifts you give don't have to be extravagant, but you must act proud while presenting them. When you receive a gift, ask permission to open it. An item that represents your country, candy, and books are all appropriate gifts. They prefer gifts from the United States, such as special hand-crafted items or Native American items. Flowers that you should not give are chrysanthemums, because they're the national flower and because they are used at funerals. You don't want to give camellias, lotus blossoms, and lilies either, because they too represent death.

Usually the Japanese department store where you purchase your gift will wrap it. Most department stores will send your gift, so be sure to include your name on the package. In Japan the recipient usually checks with the department store that wrapped the gift to get an idea of how much to spend for a reciprocal gift. Wrap the gift neatly, without wrinkles. Decorate with red and white or gold and red cord for ordinary occasions, business openings, birthdays, and so forth.

A special paper cord called *mizuhiki* is used only for certain special occasions. Gold and silver cord are reserved for weddings. It is typical to give money as a wedding gift. Usually a guest tries to give enough money to cover the costs of the meal at the reception. The money is given in special envelopes that are presented at the reception when signing the guest register. If you want to send a gift, this is fine.

Attire

Conformity, even in appearance, is a characteristic of the Japanese. The general rule is to act similar to, or in harmony with, the crowd. Conservative dark blue or gray suits with a white shirt and tie are the staples of Japanese business attire for men. Men should never wear brightly colored ties. Similarly colored suits or dresses are appropriate for women. Men, if you're going to be attending formal affairs, leave the tuxedo at home and bring a dark suit and tie instead. Women, plan to wear a cocktail or evening dress. To be most comfortable and prevent any embarrassing incidents from occurring while sitting on the floor when dining, the clothes you bring should fit loosely. Flashy or loud clothing is frowned upon.

It is common for people who have infectious diseases, such as a cold or the flu, to wear protective masks over their mouth and nose. Don't be too worried when you see this; it is done for your protection.

Transportation

Even though Japan has a highly developed, efficient mass-transit system of trains and buses, transportation can be a problem. Still, getting cabs at a hotel is simple. The cabs are kept meticulously clean and well maintained, but many drivers do not speak English. However, it is also possible to hire English-speaking drivers.Unless you can read the language, public transportation can be difficult to use, because most of it is written in *kanji* characters. And the subway is extremely crowded. As with all travel you'll have to be adventuresome and see what works best for you.

It is easy to get a cab at a hotel, but flagging one down yourself can be difficult. Restaurants will also call a cab for you. This, or walking, if that is an option, may be your best bet if you want to get to your appointments on time. Carrying your hotel card and another card with your destination written in Japanese on it will be especially helpful when traveling anywhere in Japan.

CHINA

American companies are doing more business with China. You may one day find yourself doing business with the Chinese, taking a trip there, or living there to work. Thus, it is important that you know about the country's customs, culture, and traditions. If your trip also includes Taiwan, much of this information will be helpful to you as well, as most customs in China and Taiwan are very similar.

Chinese culture, by virtue of its history, has always been based upon stability and splendor. This is vastly different from Western and American culture, which embraces change and sometimes encourages revolution. These differing viewpoints and cultures make it especially important for natives of the two countries to understand and accept one another. Therefore, before traveling to China, you must study its culture and learn to respect it. The Chinese abide very closely by their culture's rules and are more likely to accept you and trust you if you have learned those rules. An "Introduction to China 101" course isn't going to be enough. You will need to be knowledgeable enough about their festivals, art, calligraphy, language, literature, religion, family lifestyles, customs, handicrafts, and cuisine to hold at least a simple conversation on any one or all of these areas.

Greetings

When you meet your Chinese business associate or any other Chinese individual for the first time, display your respect for him by nodding your head and bowing slightly. A handshake is also acceptable, especially in formal situations or to show respect. A greeting common to foreigners is *Ni hao ma?* (How do you do?). While many Chinese accept this terms and use it, there are also various, more traditional terms. A common informal greeting is *Chi le ma?* (Did you eat?). The response is either *Chi le* (Yes) or *Mei you* (Not yet).

You'll avoid making a common social blunder if you remember that in China, the order of people's names is opposite that in the United States. In other words, when a Chinese person tells you his name, the first name he says is his last name or family name, which has one syllable, and the second name he gives is his first or given name, which has two syllables. Always address your Chinese associate by his business title—chairperson, president, and so forth. Addressing a person as Mr., Mrs., or Ms. is disrespectful. Although it has just recently become socially acceptable in the United States for a married woman to retain her maiden name, this practice is customary in China. Be sure to keep this in mind when you address your business associate's wife, and always include a person's family name when addressing her by her formal or professional title. Whenever you are in the company of people of various ages, always greet and speak to the older people first. When you are the guest at a large banquet, it's up to you to introduce yourself to others sharing your table.

The Chinese language is complex and contains many dialects that are not all interchangeable. What may make it even more difficult for a foreigner to learn the language is that it contains very few rules of grammar. Rote memorization is the only way to learn the thousands of characters that make up the language. And although each character's meaning is the same in all the dialects, each dialect pronounces them differently. This means that drawing characters may be necessary when conversing with someone who speaks a dialect with which you are not familiar.

Politics is a subject the Chinese don't like to talk about, so it's best not to bring it up. Children enjoy answering questions about their schoolwork, and elderly people are not offended when you inquire about their health.

Yes, *no*, and *maybe* can be particularly troublesome words when speaking with a Chinese person, because they have different meanings in Chinese than they do in English. *Yes* often conveys understanding, not agreement, whereas *maybe* most often conveys disagreement. Because the Chinese find disagreeing very impolite and don't want to offend anyone, they will say yes to an appointment even if they know they can't be there. When your associate says yes, she may mean that she will meet you at the appointed time and place, or that she would like to meet you, but at another time (she won't say this, though). If she doesn't show up, don't be offended. Continue to try to find a time she is available. Clarification may be necessary when using the words *yes*, *no*, and *maybe*.

The Chinese are skilled bargainers. Knowing how well the person you're dealing with speaks and understands English can prevent you from losing a deal. In an attempt to wear you down, your counterpart may pretend that he doesn't understand what you're saying, and he may ask you to repeat your presentation or have it translated into his language. This also gives him time to think of a response.

Social Graces

When in public, be reserved and refrain from displaying affection. This includes kissing, hugging, and even winking. Avoiding eye contact is a sign of respect. Don't put your arms around other people's shoulders. Except in crowds when physical contact is unavoidable, the Chinese do not like to be touched by people they do not know. The Chinese use their open hand to point rather than one finger. To beckon, all fingers wave with the palm of the hand facing down. Eating while walking down the street is inappropriate, as it is in most other countries, including the United States. When criticizing another, make your comments constructive, not hurtful. While you're seated, place your hands in your lap, and no matter how much of a habit it is, don't jiggle your legs. It's fine for women to sit with their legs crossed, but neither sex should use their legs or feet to move objects such as chairs or to shut doors.

Business Matters and Business Cards

The typical Chinese business day goes from 8:00 A.M. to noon and 2:00 P.M. to 6:00 P.M., Monday through Saturday. Banks and government offices have similar hours. Shops are open from 9:00 A.M. to 7:00 P.M. every day. Restaurants run by the State often close by 8:00 P.M.

If you have access to a newer phone, you can make international calls directly. If you don't, you'll have to dial 100 to get assistance from the international operator. The information revolution has brought satellite disks, fax machines, and electronic mail to China.

Before you meet with your counterpart, be sure he receives your letter of introduction stating who you are, the name of the company you work for, and your business and family background. This letter must be prepared by someone who knows you both, such as a business associate or friend, or by a bank officer. When you are introduced, have your business card ready, one side printed in English, the other in Chinese. To gain trust in you, your counterpart will put you to the test. His evaluation of you as a person rather than anything that's written on paper in contracts and agreements, is more important, and more of a factor, in his decision to accept your deal. To win his trust, you must promote yourself, earn his respect and understanding, be observed in a variety of situations that prove your business associates trust and think well of you and, develop a friendly, nonbusiness relationship with your counterpart outside the office. Remember too that business is mostly for males. You will probably want to ask before bringing your wife to the after-work get-together.

Be prepared for long bargaining sessions. The Chinese bargain for almost everything, and business is no exception. You may be asked how much you paid for various items, such as clothing and jewelry. This gives them an idea of their bargaining power and the value of items. You are expected to do the same. Remember that patience is a virtue, and when dealing with the Chinese, you're going to need all the patience you can muster. They don't rush into any decisions. If your counterpart knows your deadline, he will use it to his advantage. Giving a phony deadline may help you get the results you need before your actual deadline. Limit the amount of information you divulge, and for as long as possible. Also be aware that confidentiality is not always guaranteed.

Business Attire

Chinese business attire is essentially the same as that in the United States; the standard suit and tie for men and dress or skirt and blouse for women. This is also proper dress for other occasions, such as when dining at someone's home or at a restaurant. Having food all over your clothes and the tablecloth when dining is the sign of a good meal. Accordingly, you may not want to wear your expensive new suit. Wash-and-wear clothing is best to take, as modern cleaning facilities are not always available. If diplomatic functions are on the agenda, men must have their tuxedos handy. Women should wear a full-length dress.

Entertaining

Invitations are usually extended for formal occasions, but otherwise it is common to drop by unannounced. When invited, one is generally prompt. Being more than a few minutes late is impolite.

Very little business entertaining done in China is done in private homes. It is becoming more common now to entertain in private homes than it has been previously, but it still is not standard practice. When entertaining is done in the home, do not be offended if your host's wife doesn't join you. Her place is in the kitchen, preparing your meal. It is appropriate to bring a gift, such as high-quality tea or candy, to your host, but don't bring one that is far above your host's income level. The Chinese feel they must give you a gift of equal or higher value, and if you give them something that costs a great deal, they may have a difficult time matching it.

The English phrase for "Give a clock" and the Chinese phrase for "Watching someone dying" sound very much alike. Therefore, saying this can give a Chinese person the impression that you're cursing another or wishing him dead. Also, giving a clock as a gift is believed to bring bad luck to the recipient, so avoid giving clocks as gifts. And if you give flowers, remember that white flowers symbolize mourning and colorful flowers are appropriate only for weddings.

Present your gift with both hands, but don't be offended if it is not opened in your presence. To save the giver from being embarrassed if the gift is inappropriate, gifts aren't opened in the presence of the giver. Be sure to remove your shoes before you enter the house, and put on the slippers provided by your host. Your host will verbally demean himself and his home, and no matter how unusual or uncomfortable it may seem to you, you must respond by demeaning yourself and complimenting him. Don't lavishly praise his possessions, though; he will feel obligated to give them to you.

When the Chinese entertain in their home, a banquet-style meal is usually served. When your host announces that the meal is ready, show reluctance and enter the dining room when the other Chinese guests do. There may or may not be a tablecloth on the table, and there won't be any napkins. Hot towels are used instead. Speeches and toasts will be given before the meal is served. The utensils in your place setting will consist of chopsticks and a spoon. Knives aren't necessary, because your food is served in bite-sized pieces. It's fine to ask for a fork if you just can't get the hang of using chopsticks.

When the host apologizes for the quality of the meal you're about to eat, don't worry. This self-effacement is customary. Your duty as a guest is to compliment him and tell him he's being modest. He may apologize again for the meal at its conclusion. Complimentary responses are in order here also. If your host takes a piece of food from his plate and places it on your plate, don't ask him what's wrong with it and don't ask why he doesn't want it. This is his way of honoring you as a guest. The appropriate response is to thank him.

Beverages and Toasts

The Chinese tend to consume large amounts of alcohol, and make toasts during festive occasions. Most often, sherry-flavored

Shaohsing or fiery Kaoliang wine is the beverage served. Wine is served warm and in small cups. To drink from the cup, hold one hand under it with the other wrapped around it, and unless you hear "Kan-bei," which means something like "dry cup" or "bottoms up to you and me," you can take just small sips. Beer, hot water, cognac, or soda may be served with a meal also. Tea is served before and after, but not during meals, and it is improper to drink tea with milk or sugar. All toasts must be returned, and so many may be made that it's difficult to keep up. And don't be surprised if you get involved in a drinking game.

It may take some time for you to adapt to Chinese table manners, because they are quite different from those in the United States. The dining atmosphere often is quite noisy. Soup and noodles are slurped, and the louder the better. Food bowls are lifted to the mouth, so it's easier to push food into it with your chopsticks. Items such as gristle, bones, and fruit pits are spat on the floor or tablecloth instead of being removed from your mouth with a fork or spoon. And toothpicks may be used at the table as long as you cover your mouth with one hand while you remove food from your teeth. Bring your napkin, because your host won't provide any.

If you take your Chinese counterpart out to a restaurant, firmly establish that you will be picking up the check, or pay before you eat; otherwise, he will insist on paying. As the host, you also must escort your guests to their cars or cabs.

Most hotel meals are quite plain. Other Chinese restaurants—and there are many different types—give you a taste of real Chinese cuisine. Expect good food, and a sampling of Chinese culture.

When you think of Chinese food, do you automatically think of rice? Most people do, but not all Chinese dishes are served with rice. You may be surprised to learn that no rice is grown in the northern half of China. Wheat is the main crop. Thus, having noodles, breads, dumplings, buns, and rolls with your meals is quite common. And rice is more likely to be served in homes than in restaurants.

Be aware of the fact that the Chinese waste very little. Therefore, almost every edible part of a plant or animal is likely to find its way to the table. Depending upon how daring you are, you may or may not want to ask what is in the food you are eating.

Transportation

All major transportation facilities are state owned. Individuals travel by train, bicycle, or bus. Domestic air travel is also available, but expensive, and not always reliable. In some areas, people travel by river barge or ferry. Roads between cities are often in poor condition. Very few people have cars.

The problem you may have with transportation is communication. Few cabbies, train, and bus drivers speak English. Having your destination written in Chinese on your hotel card is a wise idea. Carrying your hotel card and a map written in both English and Chinese can save you many hours of being lost and can help you get where you're going.

Index

Available from Brighton Publications, Inc.

Meeting Room Games: Getting Things Done in Committees by Nan Booth

Installation Ceremonies for Every Group: 26 Memorable Ways to Install New Officers by Pat Hines

Hit the Ground Running: Communicate Your Way to Success by Cynthia Kreuger

Christmas Party Celebrations: 71 New & Exciting Plans for Holiday Fun by Denise Distel Dytrych

Games for Party Fun by Sharon Dlugosch

Games for Wedding Shower Fun by Sharon Dlugosch, Florence Nelson

Wedding Plans: 50 Unique Themes for the Wedding of Your Dreams by Sharon Dlugosch

Wedding Hints & Reminders by Sharon Dlugosch

Wedding Occasions: 101 New Party Themes for Wedding Showers, Rehearsal Dinners, Engagement Parties, and More! by Cynthia Lueck Sowden

Dream Weddings Do Come True: How to Plan a Stress-free Wedding by Cynthia Kreuger

Games for Baby Shower Fun by Sharon Dlugosch

Baby Shower Fun by Sharon Dlugosch

Kid-Tastic Birthday Parties: The Complete Party Planner for Today's Kids by Jane Chase

Romantic At-Home Dinners: Sneaky Strategies for Couples with Kids by Nan Booth/Gary Fischler

Reunions for Fun-Loving Families by Nancy Funke Bagley

An Anniversary to Remember: Years One to Seventy-five by Cynthia Lueck Sowden

Folding Table Napkins: A New Look at a Traditional Craft by Sharon Dlugosch

Table Setting Guide by Sharon Dlugosch

Tabletop Vignettes by Sharon Dlugosch

These books are available in selected stores and catalogs. If you're having trouble finding them in your area, send a self-addressed, stamped, business-size envelope and request ordering information from:

Brighton Publications, Inc.
P.O. Box 120706
St. Paul, MN 55112-0706

or call: 1-800-536-BOOK (2665)

www.partybooks.com

About the Author

Elizabeth L. Craig, a career management specialist, educator, author, and professional speaker has over twenty-five years experience in personal and professional skills development. As a multitalented businesswoman she has dedicated her expertise to helping individuals and organizations reach their highest levels of success.

Ms. Craig has a bachelor of science degree with high distinction in education from the University of Minnesota, and a master of business administration degree from the University of St. Thomas in St. Paul, Minnesota.

Elizabeth L. Craig is president of the CRAIG GROUP INTERNATIONAL a Minneapolis-St. Paul based firm founded in 1982. The firm specializes in career management/employment, marketing communications, and professional speakers/trainers.

Elizabeth Craig is available for private consultations,
classes, workshops,
seminars, and group presentations.
If you would like further information, contact the firm,
CRAIG GROUP INTERNATIONAL
at
612/944-1759.

"Don't Slurp Your Soup: A Basic Guide to Business Etiquette,"
MBA Book Award for Best Business Book published,
is available at selected stores and directly from
Brighton Publications, Inc. 1/800-536-BOOK (2665)